Map of Plymouth, 1643. The Civil War in which Plymouth was to play such a pivotal rôle was into its second year when this engraving of the fortifications was made. The walled town, which bravely withstood a three-year siege, is clearly seen. So are the five triangular forts which protected it from the Royalist armies. St Budeaux (St Butok's) in the north-west corner, Stoke village and Eggbuckland (Eg Bucland) were miles from anywhere at this time, but Compton was used as a base by the invading army under Prince Maurice.

PLYMOUTH
A Pictorial History

Spooner's Corner, facing Bedford Street and Old Town Street, was one of the most favoured of pre-war rendezvous. Trams were in their heyday, as is clear from this evocative shot, showing St Andrew's church in the background.

PLYMOUTH
A Pictorial History

Guy Fleming

Phillimore

1995

Published by
PHILLIMORE & CO. LTD.
Shopwyke Manor Barn, Chichester, West Sussex

ISBN 0 85033 963 4

Printed and bound in Great Britain by
BIDDLES LTD.
Guildford, Surrey

List of Illustrations

Frontispiece: Spooner's Corner

The author wishes to thank The Western Morning News Co. Ltd. as well as the many people, too numerous to detail, who have loaned snaps and cards from their own collections.

1 A few fisherfolk formed the nucleus of Plymouth, described in Domesday Book as 'Sutone'. The tiny settlement hovered on the edge of Sutton Pool. From this has grown a city of 260,000, known all over the world. The streets leading to Sutton Harbour saw many different activities, on which the town later grew prosperous. Wine, fish and war, in that order, were the three most important trades that made Sutton Harbour and, through the harbour, Plymouth, as local historian Crispin Gill has pointed out.

2 This early 18th-century print of Devonport dockyard and its environs gives some idea of the panache which lay behind many of its buildings. Samuel and Nathaniel Buck worked together on several such scenarios. This was executed from Torpoint, on the western side of the Tamar. The lengthy Dockyard Rope Walk can be seen on the right, with Mount Wise gently looming over it.

Introduction

Plymouth owes its importance to a superb freak of geography—it commands the mouth of the English Channel and boasts two ready-made harbours. Its potential as a naval centre was recognised by King Edward I in the late 13th century when he assembled a glittering display of 352 ships, the country's first national navy, in Plymouth Sound with an army which was to deliver a crushing blow to France at Poitiers.

Plymouth's history, in fact, has been determined by the sea and those who sailed across it. Captain Cook, for instance, sailed from Plymouth on all his voyages. In 1768 he left in the *Endeavour* to sail around the world and in 1772 he sailed for New Zealand in the *Resolution*. Captain Furneaux, of Swilly, Plymouth, was in the ship *Adventure* that went with Cook on that voyage from which he did not return; in 1779 he was killed by natives in the South Seas. William Bligh, of *Bounty* fame, was a successful naval captain who, in 1787, was sent to the South Seas island of Otaheite to obtain the bread fruit plant. This was the voyage during which Fletcher Christian and a mutinous crew took over the ship and set Bligh and about twenty castaways adrift in an open boat. It is remarkable that they all survived the 4,000-mile drift to Timor.

But what makes the modern Plymouth so much more than a smudge on the map? According to the late J.C. Trewin, one of Plymouth's most famous sons, it is 'at once proud, haunted and inescapably romantic'. There is a certain pathos about the place which can almost certainly be put down to its history.

Plymouth was savagely put to the torch by the barbaric Bretons when 1,200 of them arrived in 30 ships and sent 600 houses blazing into the sky; it was soon after that mini-invasion that Henry V ordered a castle to be built at the harbour's entrance. The town has experienced the hideous, blood-curdling shouts of the press gangs, bent on their infamous work, endured the long anguish of a three-year siege during the Civil War, lost thousands of its townspeople through two fearful outbreaks of cholera during the last century and seen its heart razed to the ground by bombs in this one.

But Plymouth, too, has known its great times of celebrations. Its magnificent esplanade, the Hoe, has again and again been crowded by sightseers awaiting the homecoming of victorious fleets and ships, from Francis Drake's *Golden Hind* to the arrival of the battered HMS *Exeter* in 1940 and the return of *Gipsy Moth* with Sir Francis Chichester at the helm in 1967.

The old Plymouth area, much more circumscribed than now, was almost an island for many centuries. Water lapped the lower reaches of Pennycomequick, Marsh Mills and Stonehouse Creek, all long since reclaimed. And although its claim to fame lies with the sea, it was festooned with farms and rural tranquillity until quite recent years. Indeed, some elderly people can still just about recall the days when there were numerous farms in modern suburbs such as Weston Mill, Compton, Efford, Lipson Vale and Milehouse. Stables were provided in Wolseley Road and Pemros Road; watercress from the stream could be collected at Weston Mill to where timber was floated in barges from villages like Bere Alston. Weston Mill was surrounded by farms on three sides, many of them producing masses of juicy fruits, like strawberries; freshwater trout jumped in the stream that meandered from Camel's Head; farms lined the landscape all the way from Weston Mill to Honicknowle.

The genesis of this great city could scarcely have been more unprepossessing. Much of its present area, totalling 20,000 acres, was covered by a group of manors whose names can still be clearly traced. The king was lord of the manor of Sutton, the old name, and which included approximately the foreshore from Sutton Pool to the present Millbay, extending inland to the borders of Mutley and Stoke. The few houses were grouped around Sutton Pool and the area immediately behind it. Plymouth was described by its early name of Sudtone (or South Farm) in Domesday Book in 1086 when, scarcely a scratch on a piece of parchment, its population was just seventy.

Some fifty years after Domesday, Henry I donated the Sutton manor to one of the Valletort family who, with his successors, gave large grants to the greedy Priors of Plympton, including St Nicholas' Island, now known as Drake's Island. Gradually, under the Plantagenet kings, the Priors increased their powers and privileges, becoming thoroughly disliked by the local people, off whose backs they largely lived.

The year 1254 saw the first mention of 'the port of Plymme'; the name Plymouth came into use in the early 13th century. In 1298 Plymouth's first two Members of Parliament were sent to 'The Model Parliament' inaugurated by Edward I.

The Middle Ages saw the establishment of two important religious houses in Plymouth. The Carmelites, or White Friars, numbered eight monks in its community by 1297. From the first, their presence was greatly resented by the Priors of Plympton who held the advowson of the parish church as well as being lords of the manor of Sutton Prior. In 1303 they enlarged their convent at the north-east corner of Sutton Pool, beside the small creek, and there they lived, apparently at peace, with the church authorities for several decades. Over the centuries, however, their buildings became progressively dilapidated, being used for a time as a hospital for sick soldiers and, later, as a common lodging-house. By 1836 the buildings were in ruins and were demolished, their place being taken by Southern Railway's new marshalling yards and rail terminus.

The Franciscans, or Grey Friars, came to the scene in about 1383; their monastery was almost the last founded by conventual Franciscans in England. Their early years, too, were stormy ones. As Jennie Barber points out in her extremely comprehensive study of the subject: 'Their unique way of life, spent in close contact with the people and entirely dependent upon their alms for support, aroused suspicion and many among the parish clergy did all in their power to run them out of town'. In spite of being put under an Interdict, and the threat of excommunication for anyone who assisted them, the Franciscans remained in Plymouth at their original site, near Woolster Street and Castle Dyke Lane, until 1538, when their monasteries were dissolved along with everyone else's.

In the three hundred years between the Norman Conquest and the death of the Black Prince in 1371, Plymouth grew to become the fourth largest town in England with 7,000 inhabitants. In 1439 it became the country's first free borough when the tithing of Sutton Raf, Sutton Vautort and Sutton Prior were joined together under a charter of Henry VI, thus becoming the first town in the country to be incorporated by such a statute.

The town's development was watched with growing unease by the far older Plympton, for so long the senior partner, particularly when silting of the river prevented ships sailing to the little inland village. An ancient rhyme put it thus: 'When Plymouth was a fuzzy down, Plympton was a borough town'. In 904 it was recorded under the name Plymentum and, in Domesday Book, as Plintona or 'the head of the lake'. The establishment of Plympton Priory helped it to attain significance. The College of the Black Canons Regular were transferred there from Exeter after the refusal of its priests to 'leave their concubines'. Later, with greatly increased powers, the priests exacted from all kings of resented privileges, though in the reign of Henry I their arrogant claim to the benefice of Sutton was challenged by John de Valletorta. King Stephen sent an army to quell the rebellion stirred by Baldwin de Redvers. The castle was successfully stormed, the country laid bare for miles around and the cattle forced in droves to Exeter.

Two centuries later, the growing agitation for independence began to unsettle the loose-living Priors of Plympton who, by that time, had secured St Nicholas' Island for their own and monopolised the fishing from the entrance of Cattewater to the head of the Plym.

The creation of the separate Plymouth borough enabled the town to surge ahead in significance. By the 16th century it had 9,000 inhabitants huddled around Sutton Pool, and was the sixth largest trading port in the country. Fishermen unloaded their rich hauls on their return from the Newfoundland fisheries, while local merchants landed their French and Spanish wines, salt, paper and linen cargoes. Woolsacks and ingots of tin and lead stood near the quays, ready for export.

Its nautical links were very strong from the first, not least because the Navy had been victualled from Sutton Harbour for centuries. In 1470 the Earl of Warwick and the Duke of Clarence landed at the port, starting the revolt which led to the temporary restoration of Henry VI. In the following year it was the landing place of Henry's queen, Margaret of Anjou. With the discovery of America in 1492, Plymouth assumed a greater importance; many epic voyages of discovery started from Sutton Harbour. The names of their leaders read like a roll-call of Elizabethan nautical honour: Richard Hawkins and his son John, 'Father of the Royal Navy'; Humphrey Gilbert, who took the first European settlers to North America and who later opened up Newfoundland; Walter Raleigh, famed for his exploration of Virginia; Richard Grenville, who died fighting a Spanish fleet with his ship, *The Revenge*; Martin Frobisher who pioneered the navigation of the North-West Passage. The English fleet was concentrated at Plymouth when Henry VIII landed at the head of the Allied force in the north of France, and Edward Howard, the Lord High Admiral, awaited the old enemy's movements in the Cattewater. Eventually, he pursued 15 French sail of the line. Later, the tables were turned and it was left to his brother, Thomas, to rally the thoroughly demoralised sea-force. Some of the deserters were hung from a gallows on the Hoe. Plymouth's name will always be linked with Sir Francis Drake, the pirate adventurer who circumnavigated the globe in 1580 and who played a decisive rôle in the defeat of the Spanish Armada eight years later. Sir Humphrey Gilbert sailed from Plymouth in 1583 in his abortive attempt to found a settlement on Newfoundland. Later, Sir Walter Raleigh sent out an expedition from Plymouth to explore Pamlico Sound; it was thus the happy lot of Plymouth sea-farers to discover that country where 'man lived after the manner of Golden Age', and which Queen Elizabeth named Virginia.

The Pilgrim Fathers sailed from Plymouth to New England in the *Mayflower* in 1620. Many are familiar with the story of this little barque of 180 tons sailing from Southampton and being forced to put into Plymouth for repairs. The 101 Nonconformist refugees were 'kindly entertained and courteously used by divers friends there dwelling' before setting out for the barren shores of Massachusetts Bay. Those pious Puritans were the seed of the American nation and on the Barbican a memorial records their farewell to England.

In 1625 a nautical gathering of a very different flavour took place. Over ninety men-o'-war assembled in the Sound, with 10,000 soldiers encamped on the Hoe, in preparation for the king's abortive strike at Spain. The maintenance of this huge army fell upon Plymouth with crushing weight. Mutiny was commonplace; the ringleaders were tried at drumhead and shot in the nearest open space. King Charles decided to see for himself what was going on. He was sumptuously feasted by the municipality and given a purse containing a thousand marks. Later, the ragged and ribald scrap army embarked in his presence, but the fleet soon re-entered the Sound in indescribable disorder. It was only the order to weigh anchor on pain of death that induced the captains to resume the voyage. That should have been enough to persuade them to get going again but, once more, the fleet slunk back to Plymouth. By then the regiments had been decimated as if by battle, and putrid corpses were thrown by their hundred into the festering harbour. Plague broke out with victims being thrown into open graves; the town became a charnel house, the air was heavy with death and appalling silence told of abject desolation. The king and his cohorts left ingloriously, little guessing that far graver times were soon to befall them, for the old town proved to be a pivotal point in the Civil War 17 years later.

Plymouth declared for Parliament at the outbreak in 1642 and for nearly four years was subjected to a series of sieges and blockades in which 4,000 of its townspeople died. The most able generals in the king's army attempted its capture, but the success of the Roundheads in the West Country in general was greatly assisted by the valour with which the town held out against such a large body of Royalist troops. The old city walls were too close to the town for defence and new forts and ramparts were constructed along the ridge covering the narrow land approach. At various times Prince Maurice, King Charles himself and 'Skellum' Grenville, grandson of Sir Richard, commanded the besiegers. Three major attacks were flung back, the most desperate being the Sabbath Day Fight remembered by the memorial in Freedom Park. When Fairfax and Cromwell raised the siege, at the very end of the war, they were sumptuously entertained by the townsmen, in spite of the privation and hunger and loss of treasure and trade. Plymouth's steely resistance was certainly a major contribution to Parliament's victory. In 1654 Cromwell instituted Commissioners of Victualling and an efficient victualling office was established at Lambhay at the beginning of the 18th century.

The town's Puritan leanings were emphasised when it became the first municipality to declare for William of Orange, who landed at nearby Torbay in 1688. His Dutch fleet wintered at Cattewater and it was from there that operations were directed in the spring against the disaffected Irish and their French allies.

Wars and rumours of war brought into being, from 1691 onwards, the great naval arsenal of Devonport, once the largest in Western Europe. Its growth was startling given its inauspicious beginnings. In the late 17th century the broad shores of the Hamoaze contained a clump or two of houses and cottages faced, on the western side, by the ancient town of Saltash and the great houses of Mount Edgcumbe. The river Tamar, which starts as a trickle near the northern coast, the Tavy, from Dartmoor, and the Lynher, from the Cornish moors, all meet in the great basin called Hamoaze, cutting a river bed 70 feet deep into the rock on the Devon side, and giving deep water close inshore. It is one of the most remarkable natural harbours in the world, nearly six miles in length, half-a-mile across and almost completely landlocked. The only approach from the sea is a natural entrance at Devil's Point through a deep channel, some 500 yards across. Here was plenty of scope for docking and harbouring the largest conceivable fleet.

There was a growing need for a Western port as a convoy base for the Atlantic and Mediterranean trades and for repairing warships, particularly once building began of the formidable dockyard at Brest in Brittany. Raleigh had suggested a naval dockyard on the Hamoaze and the proposal was backed by Charles II; the first sods on Point Froward were turned in 1691. The early settlement of workers grew around the newly formed town of Dock which, within 50 years, incredibly, was half the size of Plymouth.

Dock was geographically identical to the ancient manor of Stoke Damerel, originally held by the Damerell family who gave their name to the parish. This passed to Sir Edward Wise who eventually sold the area to Sir William Morice for £11,000. At that time the estate was covered with brake and abounded in partridges. Its approaches were merely beaten tracks, with the mansion at Mount Wise being surrounded by a few fields; Morice Town, later to become an important working-class suburb, was a mere hamlet surrounded by meadow. By 1733 Dock had a population of 3,000 occupying a narrow strip running up from the waterfront between two walls, but within twenty years the settlement had spread north to Morice Square and east to the top of Fore Street, eventually to emerge as the principal shopping thoroughfare. By 1801 it had far overshot the figures Plymouth had taken nearly a thousand years to attain! And in another twenty years it was half as big again, with 35,000 inhabitants, compared to Plymouth's 21,500. In 1824 Dock was given the name Devonport and in 1837 it was incorporated by charter as a municipal borough and elected its first mayor.

From the middle of the 18th century the dockyard was easily the biggest employer of local labour, employing 20,000 at its peak. In the first 60 years it built or rebuilt 48 ships, as well as refitting vessels through three naval wars.

Meanwhile, Stonehouse's development was fitful. At one time a stamping-ground for the fashionable and the famous, as it expanded so the slums came. By the middle of the 19th century it was without much in the way of streets or squares—there was merely a conglomeration of alleys and courts, all of them badly drained and unventilated. Houses were divided and subdivided on every floor; staircases were dark and handrails rickety. There were neither panes nor glass on the landings and improvised doors led to makeshift tenements. Most houses were without water and there was an absence of facilities for removing refuse. A contemporary writer commented that almost every room was 'crammed with wretched, beastly and degraded creatures, swarming with vermin and wallowing in filth'. Tenants washed and dried their clothes in the rooms in which they ate, drank, slept and cooked. The courts swarmed with children who were almost naked and stagnant water collected in pools. Every third dwelling in nearby Morice Town, overlooking the dockyard, was an inn. Local government board inspectors went on record as stating that Plymouth and Devonport ranked with Warsaw as 'the most insanitary town in Europe'. Little wonder, then, that when a lethal disease such as cholera struck, it mowed down the victims, packed so closely together in their hundreds. The outbreak of this disease, twice in the mid-19th century, killed nearly 2,000 people—far more, proportionately, than were to die in the Blitz of 1941.

Plymouth's ever-growing importance was again reinforced when the Royal Naval Hospital was built at Stonehouse; it opened in 1762 and, but for a daytime casualty unit, closed in 1995 as a result of defence cutbacks. The early part of the 19th century witnessed a remarkable renaissance period for Plymouth with the beginning of extensive schemes of enlightened building and development generally. Plymouth was, at this time, much favoured in the men who were at the head of its affairs. From 1800 to 1820 there were numbered among its mayors Philip, John and William Langmead, four of the local Lockyer family—Edward, Thomas, William and Nicholas—and the public-spirited and scholarly Henry Woollcombe, whose family have made an incalculable contribution to the city's advancement through the years. The Guildhall in Whimple Street, though not an architect's delight, headed the way with a flush of new buildings in 1780. This was followed by the Public Dispensary in Catherine Street, the Custom House on the Parade, at the Barbican, and the Laira Embankment scheme. That superb architect John Foulston came into the picture in the early 19th century, designing a wide range of buildings which certainly gave parts of Plymouth a 'Bath' elegance. This included the massive Theatre Royal and Assembly Rooms, or hotel, built within a few yards of Derry's Clock and which opened in 1811. The following year saw the laying of the foundation of the breakwater. This greatly enhanced the harbour's attraction as a deep-water port free from the wild buffetings of tempest. The South Devon Railway opened a line from Exeter to Plymouth in 1849 and, just 10 years later, the spectacular Royal Albert Bridge designed by Brunel, and linking Plymouth with Cornwall, was opened by the Prince Consort.

Both Plymouth and Devonport, then still separate boroughs, extended their territory significantly in the late 1890s, though they, with Stonehouse, were amalgamated in 1914. By 1880 the streets of Plymouth packed the whole area from the Hoe to what is now Victoria Park, and east of that to the main railway line. The only gap was at the western end of the Houndiscombe estate where the Derry family lived. Tothill and Beaumont estates were also still in private hands, though not for long. Contiguous with Beaumont Park on the eastern side was the 87-acre estate of the Culme-Seymour family, which was not surrendered for development until the turn of the century. Milehouse was still in the country but Devonport was reaching towards it slowly on the other side. Plymouth and Devonport became county boroughs in 1888 and, six years later, Stonehouse and Compton were given urban district councils, and Plympton Rural District Council was formed.

By 1896 Plymouth had built its first council houses—in Laira Bridge Road. By 1901 the total population of the Three Towns was nearly 193,000, the 11th largest conurbation in England and Wales. Peverell Park and its side avenues were built to accommodate the expanding population and by 1914 the houses were reaching up to Beacon Park. In 1928 Plymouth was designated a city and, three years later, opened a municipal aerodrome at Roborough which is still there today.

By this time, the importance of Millbay Docks as a port of call for transatlantic liners was mushrooming. Emigrants had put the port on the map as far back as 1850 but, as time went on, shipping companies found it was more expedient to land passengers and mail at Plymouth up to a day earlier than their final destinations at Southampton, London or Liverpool. Few, if any, ports of call have catered for so many liners from such varied routes for so long. Many elderly residents remember the hey-days when such sleek 'crack' liners as the *Queen Mary*, *Mauretania*, *Bremen*, *Ile de France* and the *Normandie* dropped anchor in Plymouth Sound and awaited the arrival of the puffing tenders. The all-time peak was reached in 1930 when there were 788 liner calls, with 106 outward-bound ships and a record 682 homeward-bound calls. A total of 41,130 passengers and 307,912 mailbags passed through Millbay that year. During the busy period of the liner trade at Plymouth some 14 shipping companies established new calls. They joined over a dozen other liners that had re-established their pre-First World War calls.

By 1955 Plymouth's rôle as a port was drawing to a close and just eight years remained before Lloyds listed it as closed to liner traffic. Of course, the trade had been interrupted by the Second World War.

During the Blitzes just under 5,000 buildings were destroyed and 80,000 damaged; 1,174 civilians were killed and 3,269 were seriously injured. The heart of the city was torn out. In 1943, however, the world-acclaimed Plan for Plymouth was published and, as early as 1946, the council successfully applied for a Declaratory Order to rebuild on 178 acres in the first phase of its immense and long-lasting programme. The following year, King

George VI and Queen Elizabeth unveiled the foundation stone commemorating the inauguration of the rebuilding of the city, naming the two main streets Royal Parade and Armada Way.

There were many other royal visits, among them one by the former Duchess of Kent, who unveiled the foundation stone of the technical college extension in 1952. Two years later, Princess Margaret opened the extension to the Naval War Memorial on the Hoe, the main part of which had been completed in 1924. Public morale was lifted high when the reconstructed Central Library was opened in 1956, followed by the Guildhall three years later. The Queen Mother opened the Tamar Bridge, for vehicular traffic, in 1962 and later that year the Queen came to Plymouth again to open the civic centre and municipal offices.

All the time, the new shopping centre was moving into its final phases; Princess Anne opened the Drake Circus precinct in 1971, though this is due to be replaced in a few years. The 1980s saw the opening of the spectacular Theatre Royal, the Pavilion leisure centre, the A38 Parkway 'thoroughfare' which divided the city in half and the growth of port trade through Brittany Ferries.

The 'flip' side to this progress has been the devastating rise in unemployment which, at the time of writing, stands at over eleven per cent in the Plymouth travel-to-work area. This has been reflected particularly in the dockyard where thousands of jobs have been lost in the last few years. The workforce currently stands at only 3,500 and there may be worse to come.

However, the city was informed at the end of 1994 that it would regain its unitary status, lost in the local government shake-up of 1974. This has meant that once more it will govern its own affairs from the spring of 1997. The 15th-century burghers who saw the birth of this scheme of things in 1439 most certainly would have approved!

Plymouth Worthies

This resumé would not be complete without some reference to the wealth of local talent which graduated to national fame. For instance, few, if any cities, have produced so many local artists. Plympton-born Sir Joshua Reynolds, the first president of the Royal Academy, heads the list, followed by his protégé, James Northcote, who was followed by Samuel Prout, Benjamin Haydon and Sir Charles Eastlake. All of them were born in the Plymouth area.

The city has had several notable MPs throughout its history, a number of which have been outstanding. Following the 1832 Reform Act, John Collier and Thomas Bewes were the first two returned for Plymouth, followed by Richard Collier, elected three times after 1852. He was the first Solicitor-General, going on to become Attorney-General. Sir Edward Bates and Sir Edward Clarke followed, between them serving from 1871-1900. The latter, who was the most distinguished of the Conservatives who sat in the 19th century, was one of the most brilliant leaders at the Bar, and was Lord Salisbury's Solicitor-General in 1886. His exit from the local political scene in February 1900 was dramatic in that he was forced to resign by his Local Association over the Government's decision to fight the Boer War, which he firmly rejected. He died in 1931, aged ninety.

Tony Benn's grandfather, Sir John Benn, was Devonport's MP from 1904-10, his victory being hailed in the House of Commons by Liberal leader Herbert Asquith as the turning of the political tide against the ruling Conservative government. Another notable Devonport MP was the irascible Leslie Hore-Belisha, who captured the seat against all expectations in 1923, holding it until 1945 when he was defeated by Michael Foot in the Labour landslide of that year.

Lady Nancy Astor's name will always be linked with Plymouth. She won her Sutton seat in a startling by-election in November 1919 following the elevation of her husband, Waldorf, to the Lords. A tough Virginian, she became renowned worldwide but maintained her deep love for her adopted city, which she represented until 1945. The anecdotes linked with her name are legion. But the supreme hour for the Astors was during the Blitz of 1941 when daily they toured devastated areas, encouraging the dazed but defiant citizens and helping practically in a thousand and one ways.

Michael Foot finally bit the political dust in Devonport in 1955 when the elegant Joan Vickers won by a slim margin, herself beaten by a small number of votes 19 years later by the debonair David Owen.

The legal works of Sir George Treby, of Plympton, one-time Lord Chief Justice, achieved more than just a passing fame. He was MP for the borough in 1676. He became Lord Lieutenant of London and, after some years, was appointed a High Court judge. Plymouth has also produced a remarkable range of theologians and pastors. Zachary Mudge, vicar of St Andrew's church in the late 1700s, wrote *A New English Version of the Psalms* from the original Hebrew. John Kitto, born in Stillman Street in 1804, started life in a local workhouse. A cleric befriended him, saw to it that he had a first-class education and was delighted when his protegé announced that he was setting off to Baghdad as a missionary. Included in his subsequent immense literary output was a *Pictorial Bible* and an *Encyclopedia of Biblical Literature*. Samuel Prideaux Tregelles, born in 1813, lived at Portland Square for many years. His reputation in his field was worldwide; he enjoyed a profound knowledge of Hebrew, Greek and Chaldee. Tregelles formed a design for a new Greek text in the New Testament based on ancient documents without giving preference to the then received text. He died in 1875. Richard Francis Weymouth was born at Stoke Damerel in 1822; he gave the world the first translation of the New Testament in modern language, published in 1903.

Robert Hawker, a larger-than-life character, probably ranks among the best-known local pastors. Vicar at Charles church from 1784-1827, he founded Plymouth's first Sunday School in 1787 and built the Household of Faith in 1798 to house his school. In 1809 he helped to tend the thousands of soldiers returning from the retreat at Corunna in a converted barn at Friary. Hawker stood alone among the local Anglican clergy in his welcome to John Wesley, many of whose views he shared. But it was his prowess in the pulpit which made his name a watchword throughout the West of England. A moderate Calvinist, he seldom preached for less than an hour and he held the rapt attention of his 600-strong congregation while so doing. When he died, his contemporaries claimed that the whole town mourned. The youngest of his eight children, John, followed in his father's clerical footsteps. He was a curate at Stoke Damerel church for 30 years until he was dismissed by the incoming rector the Rev. William John St Aubyn. John Hawker's substantial following left with him and built a church in Wyndham Square, which they called Eldad, and which the Bishop of Exeter, Henry Philpott, refused to consecrate. However, John Hawker and his flock continued as an independent group, with strong Anglican overtones, until his death in 1846. The Church of England bought the building, dedicated it to the apostle Peter and accepted as their first minister George Prynne, of Looe, a Puseyite and the forerunner in Plymouth of what was to be a robust Anglo-Catholic witness, which continues to this day.

Robert Stephen Hawker, a clerical eccentric *par excellence*, was born in Plymouth in 1803, nephew of Robert Hawker. He wore a navy jumper, purple gloves and a yellow poncho. Once he is said to have 'excommunicated' his cat for catching mice on a Sunday! His name became forever entwined with Morwenstow, a remote, rugged parish on the north Devon coast, where he ministered for most of his life, protecting shipwrecked seamen. Hawker revived harvest festivals, wrote the Cornish patriotic song, 'And Shall Trelawny Die?' and dealt effectively with the smuggling then rife in that part of the county. He died in 1876 at Plymouth while receiving treatment for severe back trouble and after making a death-bed conversion to the Roman Catholic Church thanks to the importunings of his second, and Polish, wife.

Five of the most important of Australia's founding fathers were Plymouth-born: Capt. Tobias Furneaux (the first man to circumnavigate the world in both directions), Capt. William Bligh, Capt. John Macarthur, Col. Sir George Arthur and Major Edmund Lockyer.

Major-General Sir Leonard Rogers is not a name on the lips of every Plymothian interested in his city's history, but it should be! Born at Hartley House in 1868, he spent 27 years with the Indian Medical services, pioneering the treatment and prevention of cholera, leprosy and other tropical diseases. Even after retirement from the army he continued this work until he was ninety.

Outstanding among the great explorers was Robert Falcon Scott, another Plymouth boy. Probably the best known of the VCs was David Chard, born in Boxhill, St Budeaux, in 1847, in a house just off what is now Honicknowle Lane. As a lieutenant in the Royal Engineers he commanded the troops at Rorke's Drift on the Buffalo river, between Natal and Zululand, against 3,000 Zulu warriors in 1879. Captain Andrew Henry, another Plymothian, won the VC at the Battle of Inkerman in November 1854 during the Crimean War, when he defended his gun-battery against a Russian onslaught almost single-handed, until collapsing with a dozen bayonet wounds. Quartermaster William Rickard also won a VC in the same bloody conflict, in his case for rescuing some of his men from a bog with the pursuing Cossacks less than 60 yards away. Lieut. Philip Curtis was 24 when he won the VC at the Battle of the Injun River, Korea, in 1951.

More contemporary local notables include Olympic swimmer Sharon Davies, the first ever female BBC television newsreader, Angela Rippon, musical composer Ron Goodwin and England's first £1 million transferred footballer, Trevor Francis. Wayne Sleep, composer Ron Goodwin, baritone Frederick Harvey and veteran actor Donald Sinden also were local boys. Dame Jocelyn Woollcombe, former director of WRNS, was born in Plymouth, as was Capt. John Walker, who did more to free the Atlantic of the U-boat menace than any other single officer. Indeed, he was decorated with the DSO and three bars, and became the senior officer of the famous Second Escort Group.

Thus, throughout the centuries, Plymouth has provided a wide range of talent to serve the nation and who could have foreseen such a cavalcade of leading figures when it all began, nearly ten centuries ago, with a group of fishermen's huts huddled by the bank of an inconspicuous pool?

The Pre-War City Centre

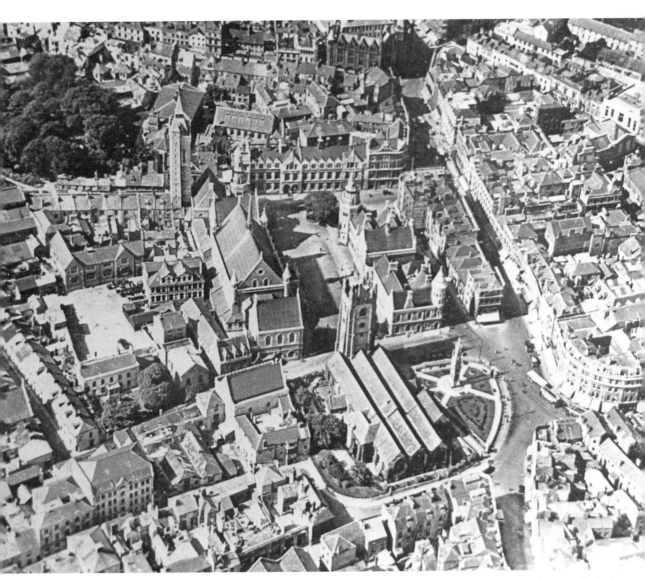

3 Perhaps the most comprehensive photograph of the old, much-loved, pre-war city centre, taken a few months before war broke out in September 1939. Within two years most of it had been razed to the ground after a series of crippling air raids which earned Plymouth the unwanted reputation of being the most badly bombed city in the country for its size.

4 St Andrew's Cross was the old city centre's focal point. Only the eastern end of St Andrew's church can be seen here, but part of the 1874 municipal buildings jut into the middle ground. Some of fashionable Bedford Street's shops are on the right, beginning with the Spooner's department store. The large block in the middle of the picture was occupied mainly by Bateman's, the optician's, and was endowed with a model of a giant pair of pince-nez on its front.

5 Bedford Street was a popular pre-war thoroughfare, renowned for its lovely stores and shops, including Dingle's. The Popham's toyroom had 2,000 dolls in stock in 1882. John Yeo's was famous for its blankets, and a popular line in button-up cloth or leather gaiters, with a strap to go under the shoe. Men from the Royal Marines Band played at Goodbody's restaurant in the afternoon and the George East Orchestra could be heard at Dingle's. The Marine Band, in resplendent attire, including horse-tail plumes in helmets, also played its way to St Andrew's church as it marched down Bedford Street for a service. Originally known as Pig Market Street, Bedford Street was dominated at its western end by the sandy-stoned Prudential building whose basement housed the Globe restaurant and grill, perpetuating the name of the old coaching inn which formerly occupied the site.

6 Dingle's at Christmas, lit up and plenty to buy! The dazzling Christmas window displays arranged by Plymouth's leading stores before the war are still fondly remembered by older people. Grottoes, with their make-believe worlds of fairies and giants, were a great draw, and each of the big shops imported its own Father Christmas—plump, rosy-cheeked and with an outsized smile. In those less crime-ridden days, evening window shopping was also a pleasurable pursuit.

7 Old George Street was a street of fashionable shops. The ladies of Baxter and Simpson millinery workroom made beaded frilled caps and satin garments. The owners used to visit Paris each season and return with samples. This was a residential street until the last century, however. The houses had grass plots in front of them and gardens behind. Hunting horses were stabled nearby. The only landmarks still existing are Derry's Clock and the Bank building at the western end.

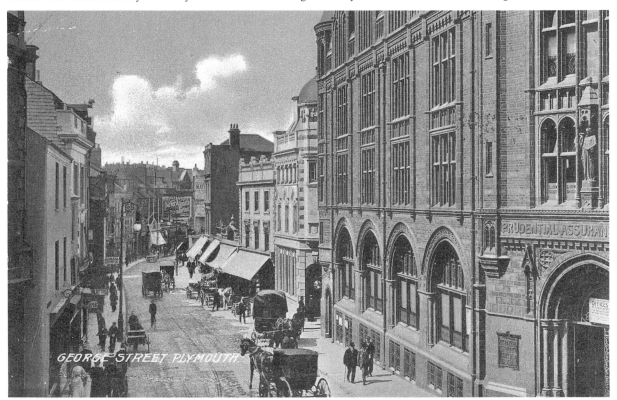

Old Town Street, Plymouth.

57298   J.V.

8   Old Town Street, an ancient thoroughfare, was widened again and again down the centuries, when it was the main artery leading out of the old town. The old town gate, which stood near here, was rebuilt in 1759 and demolished finally in 1809. It sported a main arch and stood above Saltash Street, which ran off Old Town Street. *Chubbs Hotel*, the *Old Four Castles* and the *Rose and Crown* were among the famous hostelries which stood in Old Town Street many years ago.

9   The old town junction with Saltash Street, 1896. On the far left is Pearce's Café and, next to it, Kitts, the GWR receiving point for parcels. Just down the road was Howden and Sons, which sold fruit and vegetables, then the off-licence, Haddy's. Drake Street ran alongside the Alspey store.

10 Stidson's was a huge store, a costumier, tailor and hatter, which occupied these premises at the junction of Old Town Street with, on the right, an extension of Market Avenue and, on the left, Ebrington Street. George Oliver's boot and shoe shop was next door. Part of the premises had been taken over by Mr. Jacob Best, an hydraulic and sanitary engineer, who had used it as a well-stocked ironmongery. In 1939 the site was taken over by the Fifty Shillings Tailors, the Maypole Dairy, Wray and Co., the jewellers, and piano-makers Godfrey and Company.

11 Queen Anne's Terrace happily escaped the Blitz and still stands fronting the main Tavistock Road into the city centre. The stylish houses used to be occupied mainly by professional men and their families but they left long ago and the dwellings were taken over by solicitors and other similar services. The Hansom cab, following behind the horse-drawn tram and passing the pillar of Drake Reservoir Park, suggests that this picture was taken at the turn of the century. The tower of St Matthias' church is seen on the sky-line.

12 Union Street was designed by John Foulston to link Plymouth, over marshes, with its western neighbours of Stonehouse and Devonport in 1811. This thoroughfare was consistently stuccoed and late-Regency in style. Bristling with pubs, it was an ambition for many drinkers to work their way through all of them during the course of an evening. The Plymouth police used to push them back over the town boundary at Manor Street into the charge of their Stonehouse counterparts. Servicemen arrived in Union Street in their hordes on pay night, Friday; soon tipsy, they used to be frog-marched, heads bowed, to the Stonehouse police station. The counter at the imposing *Farley's Hotel*, seen below, used to sell fresh sandwiches made to the specification of the customer and liberally spread with relish and sauces. Nearby, Sheppard's fourpenny supper shop offered faggots and peas and the ever-alert Salvation Army dispensed soup to the poor, of which there were many.

Mutley Plain, Plymouth.

13 Mutley Plain, Plymouth's secondary shopping centre, used to be lined with some fine shops and stores offering an immense range of merchandise to suit all pockets. After the Blitz it was the city's only shopping area of any size. Many of the destroyed department stores took temporary refuge in either old or makeshift properties. By the late 1980s, most of the old, well-known names had gone and now it is a forlorn echo of what it used to be, with offices and banks occupying a high proportion of the premises.

14 The name of Looe Street first appears in about 1500, at which time all that existed of Plymouth probably lay to the south of a line drawn between Friary station site and Old Town Street, east of Catherine Street and north of Notte Street. Francis Drake at one time lived at the top of the street. In the *Pope's Head* the street boasted the town's principal hotel before the *Royal* came along in 1813. The city's Arts Centre is located in this old part of Plymouth. These views date from the 1890s.

15 New Street was new 400 years ago! In 1504 it was referred to as 'Mr Sparke's new streate'. John Sparke, a major local landowner and developer, had just begun building behind the Island House nearby. New Street, shown here in the 1890s, probably is the oldest, and certainly the narrowest, of the well-used thoroughfares in the old part of Plymouth, well known by the Elizabethan sea-dogs. The restored Elizabethan House is one of the city's leading tourist attractions.

16 The Merchant's House in the 1890s. Restored by the city council in the 1970s, this 16th-century building was at one time owned by James Parker, mayor of Plymouth in 1608 and a celebrated sea-captain and merchant-adventurer. Once sandwiched between a lodging-house and an inn, the Merchant's House has been a taxi office and shoe repairer's in recent years. Today it is open to the public and features displays of Plymouth's history through the centuries.

17 *(above)*   High Street ran from the old medieval market which once stood at the junction of Whimple Street and Looe Street in the most ancient part of the town. Today most of it has gone and what remains has been renamed Buckwell Street. In the late 19th-century photograph (*left*) the men are standing outside the *Naval Reserve* pub, and the woman in the apron is at the door of the *Napoleon Inn*. This now forms the turning from Notte Street (another very old thoroughfare) to the Guild of Social Services offices.

18 *(above right)*   Opened in 1800, the old Guildhall stood at the top of High Street, replacing the Jacobean structure of 1605. Costing just £7,000, it was built mainly of limestone but included granite pinnacles taken from the old building. The new building found little favour, being quickly condemned as 'inconvenient for a Guildhall, unsuitable as a mayoralty house, inadequate as a prison and absurd as a market'. In other words, it was not well received!

19 *(right)*   Southside Street, an Elizabethan thoroughfare, was a well-trodden route from the heart of the old town to the medieval castle which stood between Lambhay Hill Street and Castle Street, overlooking Sutton Pool. The first direct reference to Southside Street was in 1591; most of the properties were substantially redeveloped from the late 16th century onwards. Nicholas Sherwill, driven from the established church, led a congregation of Nonconformists at what was the old debtors' prison and is now the gin distillery. The Huguenots also had a meeting place in Southside Street.

20 The *Old Rose and Crown* was one of a handful of Elizabethan inns which survived into the 19th century. Like the *Old Four Castles*, it was located in Old Town Street.

21 Almshouses in Church Alley, Bedford Street. Perhaps there is something a trifle ironic about the fact that these early almshouses were sited next to St Andrew's church, the seat of the mighty and the affluent. They were no distance from the workhouse in nearby Catherine Street. Plymouth had a huge number of underprivileged for many centuries, and it is still a poor city by comparison with the rest of Devon.

22 Palace Court was one of the finest examples of domestic architecture Plymouth ever possessed. It was set out as a quadrangle and its three storeys were built substantially of dark limestone. It is probable, though not certain, that the hapless Catherine of Aragon was entertained here by John Paynter, five times mayor, when she landed in 1501 en route to London to marry Arthur, Prince of Wales, who was to die five months after the ceremony. For many years Palace Court was the property of the Trelawny family. It was allowed to decay, however, and in 1880 was removed to make way for a new council school.

23 The old workhouse, Catherine Street. The first workhouse, as it later came to be known, was erected in Catherine Street under the title The Hospital of the Poor's Portion. The money came from a bequest by a local merchant, William Laurence. He also directed that 'almshouses for the education of poor orphans' be built and these were adjacent to the workhouse which, in 1849, moved to purpose-built accommodation at Greenbank.

24 The Hoe Gate was rebuilt in 1657 and demolished in 1863—the last of the eight old gates to bite the dust. It was the only one with any pretension to architectural merit, and many local people thought its destruction was a scandal. Hoe Gate had formed part of the old town wall, which, according to local historian R.N. Worth, was constructed in the early part of the 15th century.

25   In Lambhay Street, this is all that remains of the old 'Castel Quadrante' which once commanded, from its lofty eminence, Sutton Pool and the Cattewater. At each of its four corners was a battlemented tower. The building of a castle was ordered following a series of daring raids by the French. Exactly who decided on its erection is not certain, though historians tend to favour the powerful Valletort family and the Priors of Plympton. The castle played an important rôle in the defence of the town during the Civil War, but afterwards fell into disuse. By 1810 only one tower and part of another remained.

26   An old house in Treville Street, at the junction of Green Street and Vauxhall Street. It was pulled down in 1937, about thirty years after this photograph was taken. An important pre-war artery, leading from St Andrew's Cross, the street was named after the old Plymouth family of that name who had bought the Budshead estate at St Budeaux.

27 This was the entrance to what was to become Friary station but from about 1314 onwards it housed a monastery for the Carmelites, or White Friars. They built a large church with an unusually tall steeple. Gradually their influence diminished and, by 1794, parts of it were used as a military hospital just before the war with France. By 1830 it had degenerated into a common lodging-house.

28 A resolution to found a grammar school was passed in 1561 by the governing 'Twelve and Twenty-four'. It started life in the old chapel attached to the almshouses in Catherine Lane. In 1658 a new home was found in the quadrangle of the Orphans' Aid charity in nearby Catherine Street. This rare picture shows the entrance to the grammar school beyond the doorway. The 1615 motif was taken from the previous building. In 1909 the school moved to North Road where the legendary C.W. Bracken, an eminent local historian, was headmaster until his retirement in 1929.

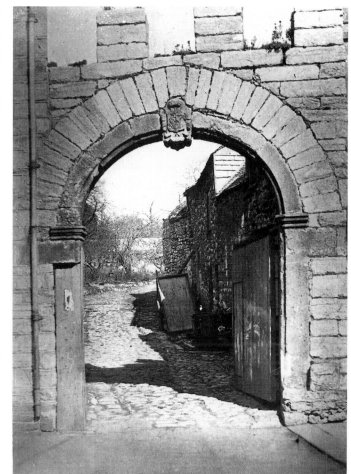

29 Lipson Road. This hill is steeped in history. At its summit, near Queen's Gate, the Plymouth Parliamentarians inflicted a decisive victory over the Royalist army, under the command of Prince Maurice, on 3 December 1643. They had taken a little fort at Laira Point, advanced around the head of Lipson Creek (at about where the redundant St Augustine's church stands) and moved up this road to the northern slopes of Mount Gould where, after fierce fighting, they were beaten back, fleeing downhill only to be met by an incoming tide at the creek. Many perished. The clash was known as the Sabbath Day Fight.

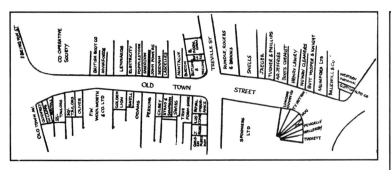
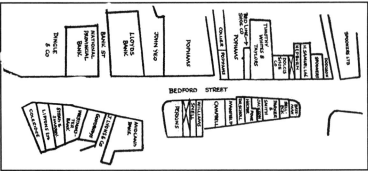
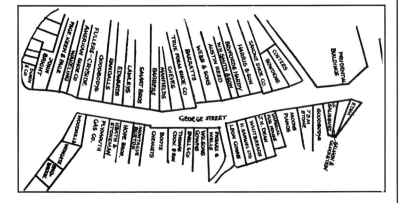

30 Pre-war maps showing shopping sites. Many of these old household names of long ago are now fading memories. Coster's, John Yeo's, Spooner's and Popham's were synonymous with the much-loved, pre-war shopping area. Their modern counterparts have been taken over by multiple giants whose names would have been unknown to the shoppers of 60 years ago. The shopping area of that time was condensed but friendly in its way. The modern replacement looms larger but has yet to win back the affection felt for its predecessor.

LONDON & SOUTH WESTERN RAILWAY TAVERN	1
METHODIST CENTRAL HALL	
WELCOME BUILDINGS SALMONS (ATW EUSTCE)	2
NEWSAGENTS	1
MADAME GERTRUDE LADIES HAIRDRESSER	2
WELCOME HALL INSTITUTE	2
AINSWORTH JN	
CITY TREASURY DEVON	3
LIBRARIES DEVONPORT	4
RAILWAY HOTEL	5
G. WIDGER PHM	6
COLUMBIA CLUB	7
TIVOLI THEATRE	8
THE COTTAGE	9
GAS SHOWROOMS	10

CHAPEL ST.

POST OFFICE	11
REINDEER CYCLES	12
CO-OP SOCIETY	13
BOOTS THE CHEMISTS	14

ST AUBYN ST.

CO-OPERATIVE SOCIETY	16
LONDON SILVERSMITH	20
& M	21
UNDERWOODS	22
GROCERS	23

LAMBERT ST.

NAT. PROV. BANK	24
LICENSED HOUSE	25
TRUE FORM	26
MORRIS RADIO	23
RICHARDS SHOES	28
CURRYS CYCLES	29
LLOYDS BANK	30 31
SNELL & CO	32
MAYPOLE DAIRY	33
GEO OLIVER	34 35
J.C. TOZER	36 37

TAVISTOCK ST.

PRINCE GEORGE PH	38
WOOD & TOVER	39
F.W. WOOLWORTH	40 41
STEAD & SIMPSON	42
STUMBLES OUTF	43
POTE & SONS OUTFITTER	44
LEY TOBACCNST	45
E.E. VENN BUTCH	46
M'SWEENEY (FRIED FISH)	47
WM LAMEY (FRUIT)	48
SPEEDY SHOE SERVICE	49
SACCONE & SPEED LTD	50
SPANISH VICE-CONSULATE (EG HATHAWAY VICE CONSUL)	

CATHERINE ST.

ROYAL SAILORS REST	56
AND INSTITUTE	59
DOCK GATES	
QUEEN STREET	

FORE STREET

119	NORMAN CAMPBELL CONFECTIONER	
117	EI-KNIT WEAR WOOL SHOP	
117	ALBERT PENGELLY LTD. TOBACCN'T'S	
117	Mrs K. DRISCOLL CONFECTIONERS	
	THE ELECTRIC THEATRE	

HIGH ST.

116 115 114	MILITARY HOTEL P.H.
	HOCKING PIANOS
	SITE FOR FORUM CINEMA
110	SINGERS
109	DAVID GREIG
109A	LEON PAGE FRUIT
108	SAM DONG DRESS
107	HEARNE & T MILLER
106	SALMON & GLUCKSTN

ST. AUBYN ST.

105	HOTEL
104	MILLBAY CLNRS
103	OWEN BAKER
102 101 100	MARKS & SPENCER
99	MIDLAND BANK
98	J. & M. STONE
97	MONTAGUE
96	BURTON

LAMBERT ST.

95	PATRICKS VAULTS
94	LIPTONS
93	TIM. WHITE
92	H WILLIAMS FANCY GOODS
91	GOLDEN LION P.H.
90	WESTERN NEWS
89	G BATEMAN OPT
88	TWO TREES PH
87	COOMBES
86 85 84	J.C. TOZER

MARLBOROUGH ST.

83	HEPWORTHS
82 81	BRITISH HOME STORES

MORICE STREET

78	COOMBES IRON MNGR
77	ROYAL HOTEL
76	TOWLSON NEWSAG
75	JEAN D PHNITY WINE
74	PAYNE'S VAULTS

KING ST.

73	BARCLAYS BANK
71	NEW LONDON INN
69 67	SYDNEY LANE JN DINING ROOMS
66	DAVID SALE LTD IRONMONGERS
65 63	
62	Mrs F WALLER CONFECTIONER

Devonport and Stonehouse

31 Plymouth Dock from Mount Edgcumbe, 1850. The dockyard began at Point Froward, middle centre, and it had expanded enormously by 1850. The population of the town increased from 35,820 to 50,440 between 1841 and 1861. Note the many church spires dotted about.

32 *(left)*   Opened in 1769 and crossing Stonehouse Pool, 'Ha'penny Bridge' was erected by Lord Edgcumbe and Sir John St Aubyn. Walkers had to pay a halfpenny toll to cross it and carriages sixpence. Future children would know the rhyme, 'Lord Edgcumbe, good and great, Open wide the Ha'penny Gate'. Its designer was John Smeaton who, about eight years earlier, had witnessed the completion of his pioneering lighthouse on the Eddystone Rocks. It was not until 1924 that the mayor, Solomon Stephens, set this, and other toll gates, free.

33 *(below left)*   Formerly a public hall, the Electric cinema became a venue for films in 1910, long before the advent of 'talkies'. Its striking tower was similar in design to that of the market, at the other end of Fore Street, though it did not boast a clock. The Tivoli cinema stood almost opposite while the Forum, further down the road, was opened in 1938.

34 *(below)*   Fore Street. The dazzling display of shops and stores in what was Devonport's major pre-war shopping centre, still is fondly remembered by elderly people. Many nearby residents seldom traipsed into Plymouth other than for major purchases so well-stocked were Fore Street and its adjacent shopping areas. Today half of it has long since disappeared behind the dockyard walls. Only what was Forum cinema (now a bingo hall) and a pub serve as a reminder of those halcyon days.

35 *(above)* This grand entrance to the Keyham Steam Yard extension was opened in October 1853 when HMS *Queen Mary* was taken into the basin, her crew manning the yard-arms. The Albert Road Gate, shown here in 1898, was closed for the last time on 4 September 1966 and demolished the following year—its clock being moved from the left-hand tower to that on the right.

36 *(top right)* Established as the Royal Albert hospital and eye infirmary in 1861 largely as the result of voluntary contributions, Devonport hospital overlooked Devonport Park and Morice Town. In 1963 it became the Devonport section of the Plymouth General hospitals. Demolished in the 1980s, the site is now occupied by a most pleasing housing complex in which two of the original towers not only have been retained but also made habitable.

37 *(right)* 'Turkeys at 1/8d'! David Greig had three shops: one in Fore Street, Devonport; a second in Cornwall Street, Plymouth; a third in Union Street. Their frontages were identical being designed with burnt Sienna marble on white. In this photograph, Mrs. Esther Wills (née Symons, the sister of the sign-writer who painted 'HIPPO' on the roof of the Hippodrome) is in white overalls on the right of the door, facing Mr. Atwill, the Cornwall Street branch manager.

38 Blitzed Devonport. Devonport really was reduced to wasteland after the 1941 Blitz and unfortunately remained that way for years after the Second World War. This scene once enjoyed a bustling and prosperous way of life, and the temporary Nissen huts, housing offices and ships were a pathetic alternative to all that.

39 Shattered Devonport! The pre-war shopping thoroughfare of Fore Street was badly hammered in April 1941 although, curiously, two of the stores—Marks and Spencer and Burton's, seen here—did survive, only to be taken within the dockyard extension after the war, where they remain to this day, looking forlorn and out of place. Local townspeople yearn for something of their old shopping centre to be rebuilt, but precious little has been accomplished.

40 The Torpoint ferry service began in 1791, exactly 100 years after the building had begun of Devonport Dockyard. Indeed, it was provided largely to ferry the growing dockyard workforce. Initially it offered passenger boats operating from North Corner, between the dockyard and the Ordnance Wharf, and horse boats running from Pottery Quay, the present landing stage on the Devonport side. Steam arrived in 1826 and, eight years later, a steam-driven chain ferry was introduced. A permanent double-bridge service was introduced in 1932.

41 Durnford Street was named after Stephen Durnford, a 14th-century local landowner who gave Stonehouse its name. The street now contains the only significant 19th-century set of buildings left in the city. Dr. George Budd, who lived at no.1, played a leading rôle in forming Conan Doyle's methods of deduction when he helped him in his medical practice. It is even possible that the great detective writer cast his character of Sherlock Holmes while staying with him.

42 Stonehouse Pool. This impressive set of buildings, only part of which can be seen in this old print, has been described as 'the finest example of 19th century monumental architecture to be found in Europe'. The Royal William Victualling Yard, as it became known, was begun in 1826 and took nearly ten years to finish. Designed by Sir John Rennie, it gave the Navy a supply depot commensurate with its local needs. The yard and its environs are currently being redeveloped by Plymouth Development Corporation.

43 Royal Naval Engineering College, Keyham. Erected in 1879, this impressive pile of Portland stone-clad building stood majestically between the Albert Road and St Levan's gates into the dockyard. It served as the college for Royal Navy engineers for officers for many generations before this facility was moved to RNEC, Manadon. The block was demolished in the late 1980s.

Suburbs

44 The Barbican, or 'Outer Defence', was a priority attraction for tourists visiting Plymouth. It formed part of the old castle and once defended the entrance to Sutton Harbour. There were two blockhouses on either side of the entrance and, at night or in times of danger, a heavy chain or boom was drawn across from one to the other. The Barbican district was designated as only the second Conservation Area in the country in 1967. It has been greatly enhanced by a series of improvement schemes in recent years.

Signs on buildings: ONE AND ALL · 1/- A MONTH · MUTUAL · CAPITAL $100,000 · INSURANCE ASSOCIATION LIMITED · LONDON SOUTH WESTERN Rly · RECEIVING OFFICE FOR GOODS · AND PARCELS TO ALL PARTS · LONDON SOUTH WESTERN RAILWAY OFFICES

BARBICAN.

45 Barbican families for years lived near their work, and some still do. It is a separate entity from the rest of Plymouth. Sometimes there were as many as 200 Cornish luggers moored at the Barbican, which had come from as far as St Ives or

Penzance. Local beer houses included *The Admiral McBride, The Faithful Irishman, The Mayflower, The North Country Pink, The Welshman's Arms, The Crown and Anchor* and *The Dolphin.*

46 *(above)* Outside the city boundary until 1967, this lovely setting at Plym Bridge has served as an agreeable rendezvous for generations of local people. Its thick woods, meandering stream and, lately, its cycleways, have proved a magnet to those weary of urban life. Alas, it has been used as a 'rat run' to and from the nearby Estover industrial and housing estates.

47 *(above right)* In company with Cattedown, Hooe and Oreston, Turnchapel lies near the shores of the old Cattewater Harbour. It used to be an important place for shipyards. There were two here and, in addition, Lord Morley of Saltram built the first private dock in 1797. The Plymouth and Dartmoor Rail Company was in operation from the middle of the last century, while the Oreston and Turnchapel Steamboat Company plied from Phoenix Wharf on the opposite side of Sutton Pool.

48 *(right)* Mount Batten boasted a small beach within ten minutes' boating distance of the Barbican. It was named after Admiral Batten, governor of the fort during the Civil War. The tower was built in 1660 and had embrasures for 10 guns. T.E. Lawrence—Lawrence of Arabia—was posted to a flying-boat squadron at the RAF station under the assumed name of Shaw. Before the breakwater was built, Batten Bay was renowned for shipwrecks. It is now being redeveloped by the Plymouth Development Corporation as part of a massive revamp of the entire waterfront.

49 St Mary the Virgin's church stands solid and four-square in the heart of Plympton, as it has for generations. In the foreground is the site of the old priory, bane of Plymouth 'chargepayers' for many years. The terraced houses at the top of the picture, on the right, face what was Plympton's railway station, long since closed. All this land has been substantially built upon since this picture was taken; Plympton itself now has a population approaching 40,000.

50 Ridgeway was the old road taking all traffic to London. It has always been considered part of a Roman road, though doubtless made on the site of an earlier British trackway. It was probably by this road that Cornish tin was taken to the Isle of Wight and to Thanet. It has been a thriving shopping area for generations though, sadly, the ratio of shops to offices has greatly diminished since its heyday before the Second World War.

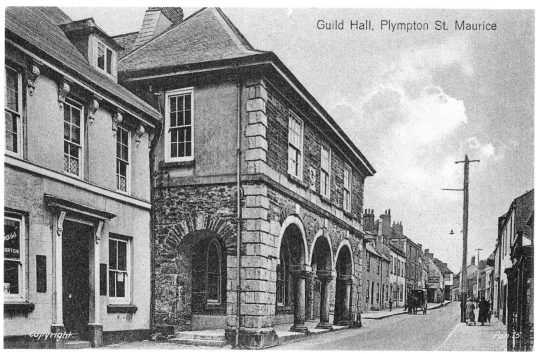

Guild Hall, Plympton St. Maurice

51 Plympton St Maurice Guildhall. The old town's rather obscure claim to borough status and a mayor was granted by a charter in 1602. Plympton school, where Sir Joshua Reynolds was educated, had been completed in 1671, and the Guildhall, built in similar style, followed in 1688. The front is little changed from the original appearance, though the rest of the building was completely revamped in 1858. Major restoration work was carried out in 1973.

52 In 1974 the *Crabtree Inn*, which had occupied one of the oldest hostelry sites in Plymouth, was pulled down to make way for a new stretch of dual carriageway from Laira to Marsh Mills. The inn overlooked the Ebb Ford (hence the modern derivation Efford) which, at low tide, provides the shallowest crossing of the Plym. Crabtree was a busy little place in the 18th century but by the 1860s, according to one contemporary writer, was 'deprived of all the bustle that thronged around it when coaches *were* and railways *were not*'. The *Rising Sun* was renamed *The Roundabout* in 1973 and was later demolished.

53 Laira Avenue in the years before the First World War. The whole area has since been transformed by ribbon development though most of these houses remain to this day. Some used to be flooded when the nearby river Plym overflowed its banks. Laira, in fact, derives from the name once given to the Plym estuary from Marsh Mills to the Cattewater. Probably it is based on the Celtic word 'llaeru', meaning 'to ebb' or 'grow shallow'—a fair description of the estuary. Laira was outside the city boundary until the extension of 1896.

54 Peverell has always been a solidly middle-class area. The great sprawl eastwards began soon after the turn of the century until, by the 1920s, it had become one of the most built-up (and liked) areas in the growing city. In Peverell's early days, Milehouse, a mere mile away, was considered to be 'out in the sticks'. Peverell was incorporated into the city boundary under the 1896 extension which also brought in Laira and Compton.

55 Valletort Road, Stoke. This is a typical scene in the more salubrious parts of Stoke village, photographed in the early 1900s. The district has always combined good quality housing with the more mundane, mercenary style. The Valletort family made their entry into local history in the 11th century, linked also with the Trematon manor and Saltash on the other side of the Tamar. Eventually there emerged from the original manor of Sutton, where the modern Plymouth began life, Sutton Prior—under the aegis of the Plympton Priors—and Sutton Valletort, or Vautort. The Valletorts were the most important of the Norman under-tenants.

56 Eggbuckland Road was outside the Plymouth boundary when this photograph was taken in the early 1890s. Now it is one of the busiest thoroughfares, leading from the Hender's Corner shops, whilst Eggbuckland itself long ago lost its rural isolation. The curious name, of Saxon origin, means 'land held by charter'—in the first instance by a chieftain called Heche or Ecca.

57 Pennycomequick as it was over eighty years ago. Up to about one hundred and ten years ago Stonehouse Creek ran inland through what is now Victoria Park and on to Pennycomequick, ending just below the railway station—a few hundred yards from where this picture was taken. The name probably goes back over two thousand years when the Celts occupied the land; it means 'where the creek meets the end of the valley'. This area is now one of the busiest spots in Plymouth, particularly during rush hour!

58 It is hard to conceive that these lush-looking green fields, on their sloping site, are now festooned with houses. St Budeaux square, now much more developed, lies at the bottom of them. Several buildings, including the shop premises, remain, as does the *Trelawny Hotel*, built in 1895, and the large primary school behind it. The name comes from St Budoc, who was a Brittany saint who founded a religious settlement on the banks of nearby Tamerton Creek in A.D. 480.

59 Plymouth joined with its neighbours in laying out Victoria Park, opened in 1891, in the old Mill Creek above Millbridge, then filled in. Until then water had lapped up to Pennycomequick, just below what is now the mail sorting office. These booted young Edwardians, with their backs to the camera, are sampling the park's swings and other facilities in the early 1900s.

60 Marches like the one in this photograph, showing Plympton Band of Hope, were all the rage in the decades leading up to the First World War. Plympton was no exception, particularly with a vigorous Nonconformist community flourishing alongside the more staid Anglican churches. The *Hele Arms* was named after Elize Hele, who had left cash in his estate for the construction of the Old Grammar school and other charitable institutions.

61 Up and away she goes! There was always lots of fun to be had at the children's playground at the western end of the Hoe—and there still is, albeit with more sophisticated facilities. This Edwardian picture shows parents and nannies watching the children enjoy an exciting time on swings made for two, with fairground paraphernalia evident in the background. The Royal Corinthian Yacht Club and the stately Elliot Terrace stand majestically on the top plateau, the Hoe itself.

62 The National Union of Teachers came to Plymouth for its annual conference in March 1910. Obviously it was not all work and no play. Here is a group of delegates, aided by local schoolchildren, performing at the Pixie Land bazaar in the Guildhall, where most of the meetings were held.

Plymouth Argyle 1903-1904

Standing W. ANDERSON H. WINTERHOLDER C. CLARK F. FITCHETT J. ROBINSON A. CLARK J. BANKS J. PICKEN B. JACI

Seated T. CLEGHORN B. DALYRYMPLE W. LEECH A. GOODHALL J. PEDDIE H. DIGWEED F. BRETTELL

63 The Plymouth Argyle football team for the 1903/4 season. The idea behind this prized yet exasperating football club originated in a house at Argyle Terrace, Mutley, at a meeting on a night in 1888 'to arrange and discuss schemes for the formation of an athletic club'. Hence the subsequent Home Park roar. Between the two World Wars, and for a time after the second, Cornwall joined Plymouth in idolising the club. The club had also formed a rugby side in the late 1880s. Both wore the green and black quartered shirts that would turn to the familiar green jerseys with black collars and cuffs. Eventually, the club rented Home Park, taking over from a rugby side, and opened with an athletics sports meeting on Whitmonday 1901.

64 'Up Argyle'—ladies' style. Some of the female supporters of Plymouth Argyle dressed for the occasion when their team won promotion to the Second Division in 1930. They started their season with a superb flourish, remaining unbeaten until Boxing Day. Promotion was assured at Newport on Easter Monday—with five games to spare.

65 A Mayflower pageant in 1920. Mostly Devonport people took part in this fulsome and dramatic pageant, staged at the Drill Hall in Millbay Park. The three hundred or so participants supplied their own costumes; the pageant master, Mr. Charles Richards, is the stooping gentleman with white hair and a smock.

66 Carnivals were much more the 'in thing' in the 1920s and '30s. Vast crowds turned out to watch the passing floats. This is the procession of decorated cars in one of the 1934 carnivals seen winding its way down Union Street.

Transport

67 Moored in the Hamoaze for many years, HMS *Impregnable* formed part of the naval recruiting establishment. Only 40 per cent of the boys who entered at the age of 14 survived the 18-month course because of the ultra-strict tests, which included manning the yardarms—no mean achievement. Home for a company of approximately eight hundred, the *Impregnable* was launched as HMS *Howe*, with 121 guns, in 1860. Note Devonport column on the sky-line in this 1897 photograph.

68 Millbay Docks. Plymouth was a major port of call until 1939, with about six hundred ocean liners a year being handled. However, the Navy, wishing for a clear run, inhibited full dock development. Millbay Docks began life in 1840, coming under the ownership of the GWR in 1874. Brittany Ferries now use it as a base for their popular services to France and Spain.

69 The crack French liner *Normandie* is seen here steaming into Plymouth Sound in 1937 after her record-breaking Atlantic crossing.

70 A favourite 'old-timer' was the beautifully-proportioned *Mauretania* which often landed passengers and mail. By being deposited at Plymouth, passengers and mail reached London more quickly by rail than by remaining on board until they reached a port nearer London.

71 There was great excitement when the prestigious Cunard liner, the *Queen Mary*, made one of her rare calls in Plymouth Sound. The Hoe would be lined with people craning their necks to see what was going on, and small knots of people would stand outside Millbay Docks in the (usually) vain hope that they would catch sight of some famous Hollywood film star who had arrived by tender.

72 The launch of HMS *Exeter* in 1928. Who among the many hundreds watching the launch of this cruiser at Devonport Dockyard in 1928 could have guessed that, just 12 years later, her epic deeds at sea were to be known all over the world. Her part in the victory off the river Plate, which led to the scuttling of the German battleship *Graf Spee*, was recognised as thousands turned out to welcome her home, badly mauled though she was, in February 1940. Winston Churchill, then the First Sea Lord, and Admiral of the Fleet, Sir Dudley Pound, came down to Plymouth to honour the brave ship's company.

73 The foundation stone of this giant bulwark against the pounding waves in the choppy Channel were laid in 1812. It was to be one of the marvels of its time, and still serves well. Its canted arms each are 350 yards long and at an angle of 120 degrees to the main part, which is 1,000 yards long. Suitable limestone was found locally at the Oreston quarry. Within a year of the start of construction, the rough shape was visible above low water mark. Its lighthouse first shone out in June 1844, just 11 years after the completion of the actual breakwater itself. A year later the beacon at the eastern end was ready. The breakwater was designed by Sir John Rennie.

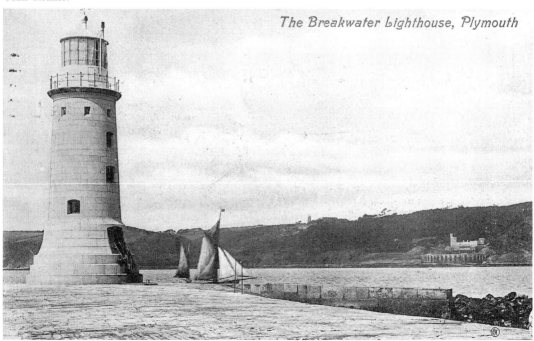

The Breakwater Lighthouse, Plymouth

74 Plymstock station and steam on the Turnchapel branch. At one point a total of 60 trains a day, bound either for Turnchapel of Yealmpton, passed through Plymstock. For the inhabitants of that area it must have seemed far too good to last—and, of course, it was. It became commercially crazy to continue. There were four stations on six miles of track between Plymstock and Yealmpton: Billscombe, Elburton Cross, Brixton and Steer Point. The latter was by far the busiest; not only did it connect with the steam-boat linking Newton Ferrers and Noss Mayo but also with freight from the fish trade. By 1930 the passenger trade on the line had faded away, but it took 'Beeching's Axe' in 1960 to end the carriage of freight.

75 The Cornish Riviera Express, the GWR's train showpiece, covered the 226 miles between Plymouth North Road and Paddington in three and a half hours, much the same as today. Its chocolate and cream coaches were striking—and so was its 'in service' and general style. This view shows the 12.30 p.m. 'up' express pulling away from platform 7 in September 1956 with two engines to help ascend the steep Hemerdon incline outside Plympton.

76 The busy terminus of Friary station was opened by the LSWR in July 1891. Built of light, grey limestone, like the neighbouring road bridge, St Jude's church and many of the houses in the area, it exuded a gas-lit charm missing from its bigger brothers. For a time Friary was Southern Railway's terminus for its Waterloo line, which travelled through some of the most attractive landscape in the whole of the Westcountry. The station closed in September 1958. The site is now covered by an agreeable enough housing development and two large, unsightly commercial sheds.

77 Yes, it was as narrow as this! Passengers could lean over and touch each other when trams passed. These two are entering Basket Street which ran almost parallel to Bedford Street, separated by the Bateman's Corner and coming from Old Town Street. On the left are the massive Guildhall and municipal office buildings, opened in 1874. This view dates from 1934.

78 Refitting at the Milehouse depot. Trams not only had to be serviced regularly but also modernised to comply with strict new regulations. Here one of the Plymouth Corporation Transport cars stands complete with its new external canopy extending over the driver's position—enabling more passengers to be carried. This tram, no.74, is sign-boarded for the route from the theatre to Devonport, one of the most used lines in the area.

79 Taken in Fore Street, Devonport in 1909, this photograph shows tram car no.9, of the Plymouth, Stonehouse and Devonport Tramways—a company which was to last from 1901-22. The original three companies' rolling stock consisted of 16 electric trams. After the amalgamation of 'the three towns' in 1914, the two distinct Devonport companies merged with the larger Plymouth one, adopting new route numbers and colours.

80 Tram 158, seen here at Mutley Plain in August 1938, was one of the four survivors which operated on the last run between Old Town Street and Peverell Corner. This particular tram was the one which left the centre at 5 p.m. on 29 September 1945 for the final run of all—to the Milehouse depot, fare 1½d. It ended its days as a shelter at Plymouth Argyle's ground at Home Park.

81 A no.12 tram in Chapel Street, Devonport, on its long, twisting run to Prince Rock in the mid-1930s. It had arrived from St Aubyn Street and, after leaving Chapel Street, would reach the 'Ha'penny Gate' at Stonehouse after passing the post office, the *Brown Bear Inn* and St Aubyn's church, which still stands, although minus it spire.

82 The trams' livery was maroon and white and the fares about a penny. Tram service no.5 plied between the old Theatre Royal, the former Friary station and, to the east, Prince Rock. The motor-bus, built in 1923, had wheels with pneumatic tyres. Then, as now, passengers paid on boarding.

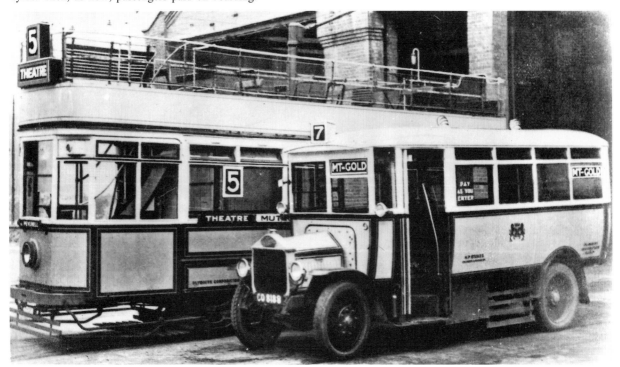

Schools, Hospitals and Hotels

83 The late Dame Jocelyn Woolcombe, former head of the WRENS, and Angela Mortimer, a winner of the Ladies Singles Championship at Wimbledon, were among the famous 'old girls' educated at Moorfield School, in Moorfield Avenue. Founded in 1850, it rapidly became one of Plymouth's most proficient private schools. Pupils wore distinctive red berets. Sadly, the school closed in the 1960s and with it went a cherished piece of old Plymouth.

84 Now a thriving independent school for girls, aged between four and 18, the origin of St Dunstan's school was tied in with the arrival on the scene of the much-maligned Sisters of Mercy in 1853. For the first year or so the community rented several houses in Wyndham Square, close to St Peter's church. Eventually they bought a nearby field, used as a temporary hospital during the cholera outbreaks. There, in North Road, the foundation stone of a permanent house was laid after the consecration of the church, generally called 'The Abbey'. From this grew the present St Dunstan's, founded in 1907. The picture below is captioned 'The Grammar School' as in the foyer of St Dunstan's is the original lintel of the inner arch which was over the entrance to the old Plymouth Corporation Grammar School, founded in Henry VII's reign and demolished in 1870 to make way for the present Guildhall.

85 Mount House school. This is the south front of this well-known boys' preparatory school, with a group of boy scouts ready for inspection in the foreground. The author was a pupil there for several years until 1940, shortly before it moved to Tavistock where it has remained ever since. Dr. David Owen was among the many boys who began their education at this school, whose premises at the end of Hartley Avenue are once again occupied by a boys' preparatory school.

86 Higher Elementary school. The original school was built on this site, in Keppel Place, Stoke village, in 1809, serving the many children who lived nearby in numerous tumbledown by-courts and alleys. It was used as a military and naval hospital during the First World War, when this photograph was taken—note the Red Cross flag flying aloft.

HIGHER ELEMENTARY SCHOOL, DEVONPORT.

1st Sectional Hospital.

87 Opened in 1903, Salisbury Road school was originally constituted as four separate sections: for defective and epileptic children, deaf pupils, an area for teacher instruction and, finally, the main school itself. Part of it was destroyed during the Blitz and today only a single-floor annex exists. The building was used as a hospital during the First World War and as a billet for troops during the Second. Well-remembered headmistresses include Miss Angier (1903-22) and Miss Oliver (1922-42) who, between them, cover nearly half the school's life to date. This classroom picture was taken in 1908.

88 The former Technical school in Tavistock Road was completed in 1892 on the site of a cattle market. It was known as the Victorian Jubilee Memorial Science, Art and Technical school, and was visited by 8,000 people on its first open day. In 1914 it amalgamated with its Devonport counterpart. The new extension block, seen here, opened in 1955 as the first instalment of the College of Further Education, now Plymouth University.

89 Beaumont House, which later became a nursing home and is shown here in 1898, was the Seymour family home from 1798 until 1814, during which time Michael Seymour won much fame and a baronetcy in single-ship actions. His son, John, married Elizabeth Culme, whose family were neighbours at Tothill. When she died in 1841, Sir John took the name of Culme-Seymour. Both names survive in the Mannamead district on former Culme land. The estates were not turned over for development until the end of the 19th century.

90 St Elizabeth's House of Rest—an Anglican Order of Sisters began its Plymouth witness here in 1879. The order returned to the area, after a long absence, in 1994 when it again set up its Mother House at Plympton. Amberley House (pictured), its original base near Plympton's Ridgeway shopping centre, is now a residential home. This time, the nuns took over Erle Hall, on the edge of the ancient St Maurice parish, which also had been renamed St Elizabeth's House.

91 The foundation stone of Greenbank Hospital was laid in 1881 by the 4th Earl of Mount Edgecumbe. The cost of the original development, which received various accretions through the years, was a mere £38,000. The South Devon and East Cornwall Hospital, as it was originally named, replaced the first public hospital, opened on the corner of Sussex Street and Notte Street in 1840. At its peak, this could cope only with an average of 55 patients at any one time. In contrast, the new hospital, which later went by the name of Greenbank, had room for 130 beds. The whole project had been made possible thanks largely to two of the great local families—the Edgecumbes and the Lopes, of nearby Maristow. Greenbank was closed in 1994, and its services transferred to the extended Derrisford Hospital. The site is likely to be sold.

Royal Hotel, Plymouth

92 Work on this magnificent building, the *Royal Hotel*, together with the Assembly Rooms and the Theatre Royal, was begun in 1811 from designs by John Foulston. It was completed two years later at a cost of £60,000, having been built on the site of some cherry gardens. It was 'the place' to wine and dine for many but was an almost inevitable casualty of the 1941 Blitz. For many years its site was occupied by a small and rather bleak car park.

93 The stately *Continental Hotel* opened in 1875 as the *Albion*, its purpose being to offer accommodation to the many passengers using the GWR railway terminus at Millbay station, only a few yards away. Expansion followed in succeeding years and in the early 1900s the whole site was redeveloped to produce the striking building seen there today. The name Albion survived until the early 1930s. In 1974 the hotel fell into the hands of receivers and its future looked distinctly bleak until, three years later, it was bought by the Plymouth Hotel Company—the same firm that had set up the *Duke of Cornwall Hotel* almost opposite. In 1984 it changed hands once more, this time to the Hajiyianni brothers, who spent over a million pounds restructuring and restyling the interior of this prominent city landmark and rechristening it the *New Continental Hotel*.

94 Built in 1865 by Mr. John Pethick, the *Duke of Cornwall Hotel* was commissioned by railway directors who were at the same time responsible for the erection of what is now the *New Continental Hotel*. One of the few remaining old buildings of real distinction left in the city centre, 'the Duke' still evinces an attractive old-style elegance. It has profited from the building of Plymouth Pavilion's leisure centre over the road and, after several difficult decades, looks set for the future. At one time the 8,000-seater Drill Hall was almost adjacent.

95 The *Globe Hotel* was demolished at the turn of the century to make way for the sandstone-covered Prudential building, a prominent landmark until it, too, was taken down after the Second World War. The city's medieval Frankfort, or West, Gate had been adjacent to the *Globe* until 1783.

Churches

96 St James the Less church stood behind the massive pile comprising the *Duke of Cornwall Hotel*. Consecrated in 1861, it was not fully completed until 1789. During the war it fell victim to the same series of bombing raids that devastated dozens of Plymouth churches. It was rebuilt after the war on the Ham estate and the site is now the home of a primary school.

ST. PAUL'S CHURCH, DEVONPORT.

97 Just across Morice Square from the Baptist chapel stood the church of St Paul's, also destroyed in the Blitz. Formed as a parish in 1846, the foundation stone was laid in July 1849 and services were held on the site even as the building was being erected. The design, with the tower and spire rising to 104 ft., was the work of Mr. John Piers St Aubyn. The parish was served by St Aubyn's after the church had been destroyed.

98 Mutley Baptist church, erected in 1869, draws by far the largest evangelical following in the city. Costing nearly £8,000 to build, it fronts onto Mutley Plain, one of Plymouth's main thoroughfares. The front elevation consists of 'a pediment over a large arched recess flanked by two quasi-towers with high pitched truncated slate roofs'. This 1938 view shows a comparatively deserted Mutley Plain; these days traffic is much more frenetic.

99 The architect for the once 'fashionable' St Paul's church, opened in 1831, was John Foulston, who left so much of his genius on early 19th-century Plymouth, Stonehouse and Devonport. Stonehouse experienced something of a boom about then. Following the construction of the highly fashionable assembly, the Longroom, in 1756, came the Royal Naval hospital, 1762, the Royal Marine Barracks, 1783, and the massive Royal William Victualling Yard, 1835. Officers and their families would have formed a significant number of worshippers at St Paul's; these days it caters more for the neighbouring bedsit land.

100 St Peter's church, Wyndham Square became the first church in England to restore and maintain Holy Communion. Its early years were passed in the white-heat of intense religious bigotry. The Rev. John Hawker, the famous Robert Hawker's son, had been curate at Stoke Damerel church for nearly thirty years when the new vicar, the Rev. William John St Aubyn, gave him six weeks' notice. However, his many admirers built an Episcopal chapel especially for him, and this is now St Peter's. It opened in March 1980 and is now one of the city's major Anglo-Catholic causes.

101 The door of the new King Street church, now known as Wesley Methodist, was opened on 4 December 1957 and dedicated by the Rev. Harold Roberts, President of the Methodist Conference that year. The original King Street church, with a seating capacity for 1,600, had been built on a site between the former market and Frankfurt Gate at a cost of under £12,000. It opened in 1866 with a prayer meeting attended by 700 people and was to become known as 'the Cathedral of Western Methodism'. Its Sunday School numbered five hundred.

Old Houses

102 Widey was first recorded by name in 1590 when Sir Francis Drake built two mills in the area when he was building the leat to bring water from the moors into the town. Widey Court's main claim to fame, however, was as the headquarters of Prince Maurice and, later, King Charles I, during the Civil War siege of Plymouth. Rebuilding and enlargements were carried out in the following centuries but it finally met its end in 1954 and was demolished to make way for Widey Primary school. It had been used by the Navy, police and the city stores during the Second World War and its demolition has been greatly regretted by subsequent generations.

103 Houndiscombe Farm. The local Sherwill family owned the Houndiscombe estate, which stretched from the west of Mutley Plain from North road East to Ford Park. Former city librarian Bill Best Harris points out that the place-name first appeared in 1244 when it meant 'the valley of the hounds'. The valley would be the one containing in part the railway line and ending at where the postal sorting office now is. It would have been a natural place for hunting dogs, though it was covered with residential development many years ago. It was demolished in 1904, at which time it belonged to the Derry family.

104 Standing just north-east of the present St Jude's church and looking down Tothill Creek to the Laira and the woods of Saltram, Tothill House was one of the most pleasant houses in the area. A Plympton farmer, Anthony Culme, leased 28 acres of it in 1680 and, 10 years later, his son bought it outright. By 1730 the Culme estate included Mannamead and Little Efford and when the last Culme died in 1804 the family also owned Freedom Fields, most of Lipson, Compton and Laira.

105 This impressive building is Cookworthy's House, named after William Cookworthy, the discoverer of china clay and subsequent porcelain-designer. Built during the reign of Queen Anne, the house attained the status of being a mayoralty house when Isaac Foot senior held office in 1883. Cookworthy, who lived from 1705-80, enjoyed a vigorous social life. It was here that he entertained Capt. James Scott, Dr. Zachariah Mudge, Dr. Johnson and other worthies, under the auspices of his Otter Club.

People

106 A gentle and gracious man, George Prynne's ministry in Plymouth lasted more than fifty years, all of them spent at St Peter's, Wyndham Square. When he arrived in 1848, Queen Victoria had already been on the throne for 10 years and by the time he died, in 1903, King Edward VII was in the second year of his reign. Prynne was a product of the Oxford Movement—a group of Anglican clergymen who tried to restore their church to its historic spirituality (as they saw it) and rid it of a weak and worldly spirit. They were misunderstood and misrepresented, and Prynne was no exception. His ministry in Plymouth became one of the most controversial ever known. However, he endeared himself to friend and foe by his gentle courtesy and unstinting efforts to alleviate acute social distress.

107 That Miss Lydia Sellon was an autocrat there can be little doubt. For all that, the Sisters of Mercy, which she founded in Plymouth, carved out a permanent niche of respect and affection from townspeople after an initial period of misunderstanding and recrimination. Local people were won over by the heroic manner in which the Sisters tackled the appalling social conditions and problems, not least during the great cholera outbreaks in the 1850s and '60s. When Miss Sellon died in 1876, at the age of 54, Christians were united in their tributes to her as one of the most consequential spiritual leaders the town had ever known.

108 As elsewhere, the Salvation Army were greeted with great hostility, verbal abuse and even physical attack when they 'invaded' Plymouth in the 1870s. Everything about the early Salvationists had a rip-roaring 'Irishness' about it. Their evangelists would have an audience cringing in fear of judgment one moment and bursting their sides with laughter the next. But they prospered. This unusual view of the Plymouth Congress Hall's violin band was taken outside the Congress Hall in Martin Street in 1920. By then six corps had been established in Plymouth.

109 Jimmy Moses was Plymouth's first Labour lord mayor and, later, Member of Parliament. He left school at 14 to become an apprentice shipwright and in 1895 he started 33 years of continuous service in Devonport Dockyard. He joined the rapidly-emerging Labour party and was nominated as an alderman. In 1926 he became Plymouth's mayor in the aftermath of the General Strike and three years later at the third attempt was elected as M.P. for Plymouth Drake. However, he lost the seat in 1931 and was again the loser four years later.

110 John Barrett was enthroned as Plymouth's fifth Roman Catholic bishop in 1929. He was to remain such for nearly twenty more years. He did much to rally the spirit of the community during the Blitz of 1941, but he was not a notably charismatic figure.

111   The Queen of Romania was a much-loved figure in the Plymouth of the 1920s. She was the daughter of the Duke of Edinburgh, former Commander-in-Chief at Mount Wise. Princess Marie used to play with her young friends on the well-known bronze cannon which used to rest near the memorial to Captain Scott. In later years she married the King of Romania but never lost her love of Devonport. A contemporary described her as 'the really regal lady in an expensive blue gown, with beautiful dark hair'. Here she is being presented with an album of photographs during her visit to the Alexandra Maternity Home, Devonport.

112   Dr. Harry Moreton, who lived to be 93, was city organist for many years. He was appointed the Plymouth borough organist in 1899, in which capacity he organised and played weekly concerts for many years. When he took over the choir at the prestigious St Andrew's church it was down to 12 voices. He rebuilt it 'on cathedral lines' to 70 voices! Here he is seen being robed by the Mayor of Plymouth, Alderman G.P. Dymond, in 1932 on the occasion of the conferring of the coveted Degree of Doctor of Music. Also on the platform are the Bishops of Exeter, far left, and of Plymouth. Dr. Moreton died in 1961.

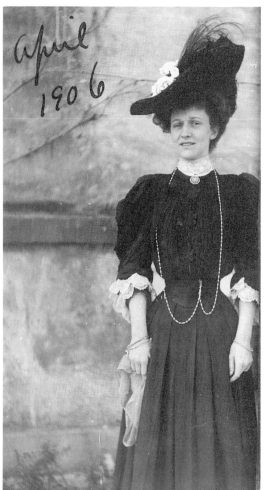

April
1906

113 Lady Astor said of herself: 'I am the most ordinary person you ever met!' One M.P. described her as the 'cheekiest little sparrow that ever sat on a doorstep'; another complained that 'she hasn't the manners of a street cat'. But Nancy Astor shook the Establishment when she won the Plymouth Sutton seat in 1919, becoming the first woman M.P. to sit in the House of Commons. She was to be returned to Parliament seven times, standing down in 1945 only on the insistence of the grave and highly-respected Waldorf Astor. He had won the Sutton seat for the Conservatives in 1910 and 1918. Following the death of his father, however, he was forced to surrender it, and his slightly scatty Virginian-born wife stepped into the electoral breach at the behest of the local Tory power-brokers. She was in her 41st year, a small, trim woman, neatly turned out, agile with quick movements, sudden gestures and, all the time, inclined to demonstrate her sharp, sometimes wounding, wit. Her first speech after her adoption meeting was typical: 'Although I am one of the most serious-minded women in England, I have the mirth of a British "Tommy". I can laugh when I am going over the top. You will not expect long, reasoned speeches from me, I hope, because if you expect 'em, you won't get 'em. I can't do it; it's not my style.' But the electors of Sutton, including a host of Labour supporters, backed her to the hilt. She never 'talked down' to them, and her rapier-like wit was legendary. Waldorf died in 1952; it was a further 12 years before Nancy followed him. One night in April 1964 she suffered a slight stroke at her daughter-in-law's home at Walton-on-Thames and, late in the evening of 1 May, she died.

114 Leslie Hore-Belisha was a former chairman of the Oxford Union, and an Army major in the First World War. He was scorned by local Tories as 'that little pipsqueak of a fellow' when he was sent down to Devonport by Liberal Party Headquarters, just 10 days before the 1922 general election. He lost the fight by a mere 2,000 votes against Tory grandee Sir Clement Kinloch-Cooke, but won it in 1923 and for a further four times until defeated at the hands of Michael Foot in the Labour landslide of 1945. A transport minister and a secretary of state for war, he is still remembered by virtue of the Belisha beacons which he introduced.

115 Her overwrought supporters broke down and wept when Joan Vickers was defeated by the up-and-coming David Owen by 437 votes at Devonport in the 1974 general election. Nearly 20 years earlier, she had ousted Labour legend Michael Foot from the seat by the even smaller margin of 100 votes. Described by one local Conservative activist as a 'political whiff of eau-de-cologne', Joan—later Dame—Vickers served her constituents superbly for 19 years. She was elevated to the House of Lords in 1974 and, at 82, received the Freedom of the City of Plymouth. She died in 1994.

Entertainment

116 *(left)* Plymouth Pier, shown here in 1912, was a real favourite with people. Jutting out from the foreshore at West Hoe, it offered a remarkable range of attractions. Many local couples first met there—particularly at the Saturday night dances. Opened in 1884, the much-loved pier was a world of its own with concerts, boxing, fishing and the start of many trips in the stately old paddle-steamers. It became another Blitz victim.

117 *(above)* The broad sweep of Plymouth Hoe is shown to good effect in this landward view. Hoe comes from a Saxon word meaning 'high place'. It is one of the world's best-loved and most elegant sea-facing promenades.

118 The old bandstand, hit by a bomb during the war, was a favourite meeting place between boy and girl, and the centre of countless sunny afternoons for those sitting in deckchairs, sucking sixpenny ice-creams and listening to the old tunes being played with panache by a great variety of visiting bands.

119 HMS *Barham* passing the pier in the early autumn of 1938, a year before war broke out. Such vessels, as well as much larger ones, often graced Plymouth Sound, usually watched by knots of spectators. I see that, on the back of this postcard, my grandmother had playfully scolded me for catching *German* measles!

120 Among the stately German liners which used Millbay as a regular port was the *Prinz Wilhelm der Grosse*, seen here in Plymouth Sound during the summer of 1906. Passengers are transferring to the Smeaton.

121　The Palace theatre was built in 1898 specifically to cater for the increasingly popular music hall acts then touring the country. This vintage Victorian colossus engaged some of the top artists of their day; the likes of Marie Lloyd, Lillie Langtry, Max Miller, Rob Wilton, Adelaide Hall and Leslie Howard were among the leading stars who performed on its stage. In common with other playhouses, however, the Palace's attractions began to wane with the advent of television in the 1950s. It opened and closed over the years, suffering many different uses ranging from a bingo hall to a night club. Its future is currently under negotiation.

122   The Hippodrome theatre was originally built as a variety theatre in Princes Street, Devonport, in 1907. George Prance was the well-known manager, much loved by the people of Devonport. Jimmy Hearn, a leading light in the annual carnival, used to allow the coach and two Shetland ponies (used for giving children a ride at a penny a time) to appear on the Hippodrome's stage during pantomimes. The theatre, which had switched to films on Christmas Day 1929, was destroyed in the April 1941 Blitz. The site is now occupied by the Salvation Army's Red Shield House.

123   The Belgrave cinema off Mutley Plain closed down in March 1983 amid much widespread mourning. When it opened in 1912 an outing to the pictures would cost anything between tuppence and sixpence and tea was often served free—to ladies only!—during the afternoon interval. The Belgrave was for a short time used as an auction hall. For several decades the site had been occupied by horse dealers and it also enjoyed a brief spell as a tramway stables. Today the Belgrave is the venue for a snooker club.

124 The Hoe Theatre. The Plymouth Corporation erected a marquee on the sacred soil of Plymouth Hoe in the 1950s. Furnished with canvas chairs and a stage, with a huge tent pole rising up from its front centre, it was used during the summer months for holiday shows. This was replaced in 1962 with a prefabricated wooden building which was named the Hoe Theatre. It seated 600 people and, in addition to the summer shows, featured pantomimes and plays. It was taken down in the early 1980s with the advent of the new Theatre Royal, a colossal success.

125 This 'blister' café did sterling service on the Hoe in the aftermath of the war and in the absence of anything more prepossessing. Plymothians and visitors alike took to it, because it was intimate and offered a wide range of food and drink at reasonable prices. The hotel in the background is the Moat House. The second picture, facing Lockyer Street, shows the site after the café had been demolished and burnt in 1982.

Plymouth Postcards

126 Even by Edwardian standards a card revealing a lady's leg was considered slightly risque.

127 This happy chap, arm crooked around one of the Guildhall towers, kicks his spatted feet in the air with delight to signal the message that he likes it in Plymouth. St Andrew's church stands over in sombre disapproval.

128 Many a romance between sailor and gal started in the gathering gloom of Plymouth Hoe.

Smeaton Tower, Plymouth Hoe I am quite fascinated by the "surroundings" here

129 Plymouth was rich with giddy little chorus songs like this in the 19th century and they were immensely popular. Union Street, Plymouth Gin and the *Stonehouse Inn* all get a mention in this rhyme, doubtless sung in many a bar all over town.

Plymouth Parody Songs.

Series No. 1.

Tune—" BECAUSE I LOVE YOU."

Last night down Union Street I walked, and to a
  maiden fair I talked,
A distance short with her I strolled, the usual tale
  of love she told,
She said she wanted to be mine, just then Old Derry
  struck up nine,
I answered firmly, I decline ; these words came then
  from Caroline :
  (Chorus)—
You know I loved you, from first I met you, drinking Plymouth Gin, down at
  that Stonehouse Inn,
When wines you brought me, and rings you bought me ; now my heart is yours
  because I love you.

B. T.

Plymouth Market Day.

'Juicy Oranges 2 a Penny.'—'Ted Weekes' Cough-no-more 1d. a packet.'—'I say, who'll have a large Hake for 4d.'—'Boot Laces, 1d. buys another half dozen; half dozen for a 1d.' 'Here you are Mum, a large stick of Tripe for 1½d.'—Ladies' hair pins, hat pins, safety pins and dangerous pins.'—'Bananas, all ripe, 2 a 1d.—(*Police*: 'Move on with that handcart.') 'Pantomime Song Book a 1d., containing Come home Bill Bailey, There's work in the Dockyard yet, So get your hair cut.'—'Evening Herald.' 'Fine fresh Water-cresses.'—'English Violets.' 'Tooth Paste 1d. a box.'—'Tomatos 3d. a lb.' 'I say, here's a beauty, who'll buy a nice young Rabbit for 9d.'—'Sold out Bill?' 'No! I'aint took enough for me lodgings yet.'—'Are we down hearted? No!'—'Let's have a drop of Gin, old dear.'   B.T.

130 Market Days in Plymouth and Devonport were almost fiesta occasions, and were enjoyed with relish by local people who knew a bargain when they saw one. The prices displayed are unbelievably low by later standards, but free dinners were nevertheless offered to the unemployed.

DAILY ROUTINE
OF A
SOLDIER'S LIFE
AT PLYMOUTH.
Set to Well-known Tunes.

6 a.m.—Reveille—"Christians awake, salute the happy morn."

6-45 ,,—Rouse Parade—"Art thou weary art thou languid'

7 ,,—Breakfast—"Meekly wait and murmur No."

8-15 ,,—C.O.s Parade—"When He Cometh."

9-15 ,,—Manœuvres—"Fight the Good Fight."

11-15,,—Swedish Drill—"Here we suffer grief and pain."

1 p.m.—Dinner,,—"Come ye thankful people come."

2-15 ,,—Rifle Drill—"Go labour On."

3-15 ,,—Lecture by Officer—"Tell me the Old Old Story'

3-30 ,,—Dismiss—"Praise God from Whom all blessangs flow." Allelujah!

5 ,,—Tea—"What means this anxious eager throng."

6 ,,—Free for the Night—O how thankful we are"

6-30 ,,—Out of Bounds—"We may not know, we cannot tell."

10 ,,—Last Post—"All are safely gathered in."

10-15,,—Lights Out—"Peace Perfect Peace."

10-30 ,,—Inspection of Guard—"Sleep on, Beloved"

131 (*left*) 'Daily routine of a Soldier's life at Plymouth.' Almost everyone knew the words of the hymns used in this hilarious send-up of British Army life. Indeed, many of them were sung in the First World War trenches, but to rather less 'spiritual' words.

132 (*right*) 'I'm thinking of you at Plymouth'—and so were thousands of other young women during the long agony of the Great War, when this evocative card was printed. Many lost husbands, brothers or sweethearts as each battle in France and Belgium produced more casualty lists. None, though, like the battle of the Bois de Battes in May 1918. There, 2nd Devons, made up largely of wartime conscripts, went down against hopeless odds and scores of Plymouth families were bereaved.

The Post-War City Centre

133 More of Plymouth survived the Blitz than is often supposed. This immediate post-war shot shows a surprising number of buildings more or less intact. Nevertheless, they were to be pulled down over the next few years to make way for the new city centre. On the left of the picture is the old Corn Exchange building, used for public meetings of all kinds in the years immediately following the war. The pile of buildings in the centre, at the head of the thoroughfare, remained a familiar landmark for many years but this too had to go.

134 Royal Parade. The rebuilding of Plymouth got underway in March 1947. Months later King George VI and Queen Elizabeth, now the Queen Mother, came down formally to open the gleaming new thoroughfare, albeit with a narrower width than Plan designers, Professor Abercrombie and J. Paton Watson, the city engineer, intended. The first illustration shows Royal Parade nearing completion. The handsome Prudential, sandstone-covered and Gothic in style, seen in the foreground, had to come down because it intruded by a few yards on the great north-south axis, Armada Way. Many were sorry to see it go. The second illustration, taken nearly three years later, depicts the building of the curved Norwich Union block on the corner of Old Town Street and, further along, the Portland stone-clad exterior of the Dingle's department store, then well advanced. This opened, amid great excitement, in September 1951, the first large store to do so in the country since the war's end.

135 Rising from the ashes: one of the most expansive photographs ever taken of the city centre under reconstruction in 1952. Dingle's, left centre, is open and the shell of the Pearl Assurance offices rises further west along Royal Parade. Behind it crouches the Western Morning News Company offices, built in 1938, which emerged unscathed from the Blitz; they are still there (at least the frontage is) but they have a different use. The large building in the central foreground is the former Odeon cinema.

136 *(left)*   As rebuilding of the city centre continued apace, many people turned against the uniformly Portland stone-cladding on all the new shops. The planners claimed there was great merit in identikit appearances, but they were challenged by developers on this point. Timothy White's hardware store was one of the first to turn the tide with the novel exterior for its store on the corner of Old Town Street and Cornwall Street.

137 *(below left)*   Westwell Gardens used to provide a lovely little oasis in the middle of this bustling city before the Second World War and for a few years after it. The park stood on the top of a graveyard and had to disappear to make way for the new civic centre. Corporation workmen stealthily removed the graves by night, for reburial elsewhere, in order not to upset any of the relatives. Happily, a number of those tall and elegant trees remain, acting as a foil to the mass of concrete and stone now all around them.

138 *(below)*   These fine sets of buildings at Drake's Circus were torn down in the 1960s to make way for a new shopping precinct, itself due to be replaced over the next few years. Only the two buildings behind the two buses escaped the attention of the demolition squads. The temporary shop in the foreground (right) housed one of the many 'satellites' rented by the Spooner's department store after it had been destroyed in the Blitz.

139 On 22 March 1941 St Andrew's church, for centuries Plymouth's 'mother church', lay in smoking ruins amidst the desolation that had once been the old city. The roof of the church was gone, the newly-rebuilt organ was completely destroyed and most of the furnishings were burnt out by the incendiary bombs which had fallen during the night. It was at this time, when the church was hopelessly devastated, that a board was fixed over the north door with a single word upon it: 'Resurgam'. Later, the ruins were laid out to form a delightful garden church which many visitors as well as residents remember with affection. At last, in 1949, it became possible to think of repairing the terrible damage. On 15 January a service was held formally to inaugurate the preliminary work. On 22 October Princess Elizabeth, now HRH Queen Elizabeth, laid a stone commemorating the beginning of the restoration. Our picture shows her doing this, watched by the Bishop of Exeter, Dr. Robert Mortimer. The rebuilding was completed in 1957.

140 German bombs almost completely gutted the Guildhall which had been opened in 1874. Sunday night after-church sing-songs were among its attractions before the war, as well as playing host to countless conferences and competitions. The statue in the foreground is of Alderman Alfred Rooker who, as mayor, led the civic dignitaries when the Prince of Wales officially opened both the Guildhall and its municipal buildings.

141 The Guildhall was Plymouth's most popular pre-war indoor venue until it was gutted during the Blitz. Although most of its outer walls still stood, it became the subject of furious debate as the city council thrashed out whether or not to restore it. The decision to do so went through by only one vote. It was officially reopened by Field-Marshal Viscount Montgomery in 1959, during the Lord Mayoralty of Percy Washbourn. Subsequent events have proved the wisdom of rebuilding this old Gothic pile, opened in 1874.

142 Building work on Charles church began in 1641 after Charles I had given permission for the new church, then on the outskirts of Plymouth. The main body of the building was finished in 1658, although the tower had to wait until 1708 for its construction. A victim of the 1941 Blitz, and now preserved as a permanent memorial to those who were killed in it, Charles church at one time could seat 1,716 people, and regularly did so when the eloquent preacher Robert Hawker occupied its tiered pulpit for 43 years in the 19th century. Occasional open-air services have been held throughout the years in the ruins. As traffic has remorselessly built up, however, it has been more difficult for prelates and people to know what was going on, and nowadays these services are very rare events. Many younger Plymothians think the ruins should be torn down, but this has outraged elderly people who value its symbolic, if lone, stand.

143 The fat stock show was held at the Pannier Market, shown here, before the butchers dressed their shops for Christmas. The mouths of pigs' heads were kept open with apples or oranges, bladders of lard as large as footballs were showpieces and there were always 'sticks' of tripe to be had. In the 1920s rice and blood puddings sold for two a penny, or seven for threepence. A bucketful of beef and bacon pieces cost the equivalent of around 12p.

144 Many hundreds of these temporary pre-fabricated homes were erected immediately after the Blitz and at the end of the war. Compact and snug, they were surprisingly popular and certainly served a useful end. The last were taken down many years after the war, to be replaced by permanent dwellings, but those who lived in them remember their tenure with affection.

Events

145 Begun in 1893, the Burrator reservoir took five years to construct. This photograph was taken in 1896 and depicts workmen on part of the site. The great dam retained the waters of the river Meavy to form a picturesque lake, much admired by visitors and local people alike. Its storage capacity is 1,026 million gallons. Devonport was not fed from Burrator until the Three Towns amalgamated in 1914. Stonehouse had lived since 1593 on a leat from a stream at Torr. Storage reservoirs at Peverell helped the 19th-century growth, but Stonehouse was glad to take Plymouth water from 1893.

Volunteer Inspection
Plym. Hoe 30·6·06

146 Volunteers assemble for their annual inspection on the Hoe in 1906. Such an event—and there were many of them—was as much a social as a military occasion, drawing relatives and friends from a very wide area. The Hoe has always provided a breathtaking venue for such displays. As long ago as 1625 over ten thousand troops assembled there prior to sailing on Charles I's abortive trip to Spain.

147 Plymouth Regatta, 1910. For many Plymothians, in the earlier years of this century, the annual regattas were the high spot in their social calendars. The Hoe was always thronged with spectators, as in this view, and many hundreds of visitors poured into the city either to take part or watch the show in Plymouth Sound, set against one of the most spectacular backgrounds anywhere.

148 It was a gala occasion when the Plymouth Boatmen's shelter was opened on the Barbican in 1933. Here, one local worthy dressed, inevitably, as Sir Francis Drake, listens to a speech by the mayor, Stanley Leatherby, whose family owned the local Coster's department store. Today, it also serves the RNLI office and the Plymouth Lifeboat Guild. Nearby, commemorative plaques starkly highlight the high casualty rate suffered by fishermen, as well as the departure from Sutton Pool of many emigrants, particularly to Australia and New Zealand.

149 The year is 1915, the regiment is the Royal Irish and the building on the right is the old *Royal Hotel*, with Lockyer Street (leading to the Hoe) in the background. This was a familiar enough sight throughout the First World War, as countless numbers of soldiers embarked from Plymouth for various war theatres.

150 Postmaster-General Sir Kingsley Wood—later to be Air Minister—is the smiling figure with a gavel in his hand. He is about to lay the foundation stone of the new general post office in Westwell Street in 1933. Town clerk R.J. Fittall and mayor Stanley Leatherby look on approvingly. It hardly needs saying that this rather stately building went up in flames during the Blitz.

151 Great crowds gathered on the Barbican in 1934 for the unveiling ceremony of the 'Mayflower' memorial. It commemorated the epic sailing, in 1620, of the Pilgrim Fathers to the New World and was attended by many dignitaries both from this country and the United States. In fact, the memorial does not mark the actual departing place of the Puritan families but, no matter, it is an immense draw to our American cousins, many of whom quaintly imagine they are among the direct descendants of those who set sail.

152 Empire Day. My generation was reared on maps of the world with the large chunks belonging to the British Empire coloured red. We were taught that, generally speaking, 'Empire' was a good thing. Certainly Empire Day in the mid-1930s was duly honoured with all the schools having a half-holiday. What to do? Well, plenty, including the inspection of giant flying-boats rocking gently in the Sound.

153 The Prince of Wales was an immensely popular visitor to Plymouth. This 1931 photograph shows him arriving for the annual hospitals' fair, one of the 'big days' in Plymouth's pre-war calendar of social events. The Prince is being accompanied by the mayor Clifford Tozer, who was later knighted, made an alderman and served as Conservative party leader on the city council for many years.

154 This view shows 'old Queen Mary', as she was then called (at 70), paying a visit to Plymouth. She had visited the town several times before the accession of her husband to the throne in 1911. She is seen here, with toque and parasol, about to tour the Greenbank hospital, now shut, in 1938. Nurses flank her as a guard of honour. On her left in his smart suit and spats is Lord Roborough, while the talkative old gentleman on her right is Dr. R.H. Wagner.

155 Pre-war generations of Plymothians were used to spectacular displays on the Hoe. These two photographs show the Service review celebrating the birthday of King George V in 1934 and, the following year, the 25th anniversary of his accession.

156 Rich in the diversity and number of Servicemen, pre-war Plymouth was steeped in ceremonies. The Hoe was the favoured venue, but the annual Trooping the Colour at the Royal Marine Barracks, Stonehouse, also drew vast throngs of people.

157 In January 1936, following the death of King George V, the proclamation of the new king, Edward VIII, was made in public places throughout the land. Here, Alderman 'Bert' Medland, lord mayor at this time, is doing just that in the Guildhall Square. Of course, neither he nor the crowds listening to him reading the proclamation could have had any idea of how short-lived the new sovereign's reign was to be.

158 Plymouth was the destination of numerous cross-Channel and Atlantic sorties. Here, the Deputy Lord Mayor of Plymouth, Alderman George Scoble, is leading three cheers for flyer Jim Mollison when he was welcomed on landing at Plymouth in 1933, on return from his Atlantic crossing with his wife, Amy Johnson, in the 'Seafarer'.

159 Another of the pre-war spectaculars at which one could get a free ringside seat was the Home Fleet preening itself with pride in Plymouth Sound. Ships of all shapes and sizes were a perennial source of interest and the annual dockyard open day, when many of them were open to the public, was something to which one looked forward for months.

160 'Ooh! You do look a sight, dear!' It all seemed a bit pointless when gas masks were tried out in the summer of 1938. They were never needed and no one believed that if the war did come Plymouth would be much affected. At school we used to sing (to the tune of 'Underneath the Spreading Chestnut Tree'): 'Neville Chamberlain said to me / If you want to get your gas mask free / Join the Plymouth ARP'. We were soon to learn that it was not just a song after all.

161 It was a sunny day in August 1945 and Plymothians turned out in their thousands to greet the servicemen and women marching in a victory procession to celebrate VJ day. It was a dazzling display which included a series of bands providing stirring martial music. Nurses from local hospitals are leading this part of the procession, followed by a naval band and then the Stars and Stripes heralding the arrival of the American contingent. The route was along Bedford Street, soon to be swallowed up by Royal Parade.

162 A partly-completed Royal Parade provided a perfect amphitheatre for the proclamation of Queen Elizabeth II's accession to the throne in February 1952. The finished Dingle's store is in the foreground with the giant Pearl offices being erected further west, and the framework of the Co-operative emporium just beyond that.

163 'Long may she reign over us!' was the heartfelt cry when the young Queen Elizabeth II was crowned in 1953 to the general acclamation of the entire population. This celebration party, in Victory Street, Keyham, was typical of dozens all over the city.

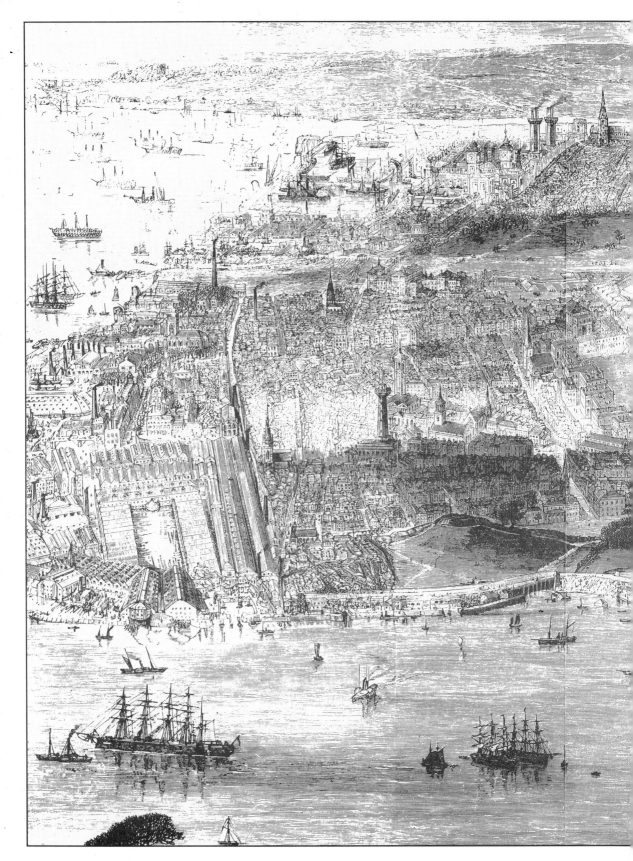

Map of Devonport fortifications.